Southern
Serendipity

12-15-06

Thank you!

Tina Rye Sloan

Southern Serendipity

◆

A Memoir of Growing Up in the Rural South

Tina Rye Sloan

iUniverse, Inc.

New York Lincoln Shanghai

Southern Serendipity
A Memoir of Growing Up in the Rural South

iUniverse books may be ordered through booksellers or by contacting:

iUniverse
2021 Pine Lake Road, Suite 100
Lincoln, NE 68512
www.iuniverse.com
1-800-Authors (1-800-288-4677)

With the exception of immediate family, the names of the characters in this book have been changed and are a product of the author's imagination. Any resemblance to actual persons, living or dead, is entirely coincidental and not intended by the author. Certain events, locations, details, and quotes have been changed. The author and publisher assume no liability nor encourage attempting any of the scenarios described in this book. This memoir was written solely for enjoyment.

ISBN-13: 978-0-595-41080-4 (pbk)
ISBN-13: 978-0-595-85439-4 (ebk)
ISBN-10: 0-595-41080-4 (pbk)
ISBN-10: 0-595-85439-7 (ebk)

Printed in the United States of America

To Clay, my friends and family, and to the memory of Daddy and Mother

Serendipity: the phenomenon of discovering valuable things not sought for
Merriam Webster's Collegiate Dictionary, 10th Edition

Contents

Part III   *Interwoven Threads*

Acknowledgments

I would like to thank the following people for making this book a reality:

Kevin Dupre,' for agreeing to serve as my editor; Willy, for being the epitome of a perfect brother; my childhood friends, for believing in me and adding a sense of adventure to my life; the families of Detroit, Alabama who took me under their wings as one of their very own; the citizens of Lamar County, for agreeing to let me share these stories; and Clay, for his unwavering support as I attempted to transform these verbal accounts into words.

Preface

My hometown is Detroit. This is not the motor city located in Michigan; this Detroit, incorporated in 1955, is located in northwest Alabama and boasts a population of a little less than three hundred. The city limits of Detroit lie within a strip of land along Highway 17, about ten miles north of Sulligent, in Lamar County, Alabama. From one end of the city limits sign to the other is a continual path, a little more than two miles.

It is a town where Southern hospitality is a given, where people greet you by your first name and wave at each vehicle as they travel down the road, and where you are never anonymous. This is a town where you never have to worry about presenting a photo I.D. since everyone not only knows you, the year you were born and approximately how much money you have in your bank account, they know your family and most of the other specific details about your life. This is a town where people still show their respect for grieving families by pulling their cars over to the side of the road when they approach a funeral procession and also take pans of turkey and dressing and platters of fried chicken over to the homes of grieving families. This is a town where men are still chivalrous and never hesitate to open the door for a lady.

In this small town, waiting is a rarity. There are usually no lines at the grocery store, the bank, or at the gas station. The residents here never even have to bother with waiting at a traffic light, since there isn't the first traffic light in this Detroit. And people here usually don't have to wait in line at the one drive-thru in town, located over at the First National Bank.

Detroit is a place where services and things come to you. Whenever people need postage stamps, they simply leave some money and a note to the postmaster in their mailbox. Whenever people need to pay their monthly insurance premium, the local insurance provider just drives up in the front yard each month, comes in for a glass of sweet tea, and catches up on the latest gossip. And if one ever needs household cleaners, you can always count on the fact that someone is sure to be selling Stanley products door-to-door.

Nights in Detroit, Alabama are literally dark. There are no traffic lights, illuminated billboards or flashing neon signs, unless you count the flashing arrow over near the Detroit Grocery. Within the city limits, there are a handful of streetlights, and to my knowledge the only business that keeps its lights on at night is the Detroit Grocery. Outside the city limits, where my friends and I lived on several acres of land, there were few, if any, streetlights to illuminate our front yards. Basically, the only light in our yards was that of the light reflected from the moon. Due to the intense darkness, the stars shone brightly and we rarely had to concern ourselves with pulling down the window shades to block out the light. There was none. When playing outside after dusk, common objects turned into hazards, simply because we couldn't see them. This is a place where the headlights of automobiles remain on high beam when driving along the blacktop, if drivers want to see more than five feet ahead.

Detroit is also a very quiet place. The only sounds you hear at night are usually the humming sounds of a window fan, the chirping of crickets, the croaking of frogs and toads, an occasional barking dog, and the gurgling of water in a nearby creek. On our remote gravel road, which was forty acres away from the nearest neighbor, only when the wind was from the north could you hear the sound of a car on the distant highway. And since traffic in Detroit is somewhat of a rarity, one could go for fifteen minutes before hearing a car go through town; even the sound of a car honking happens only once in a blue moon. In fact, the only time I can recall people honking at each other is when they passed along the highway and used the car horn to say, "Hey Y'all!" Even the sound of a siren is uncommon. Nine times out of ten, the sound of a siren can usually be traced to the local ambulance service: The Rescue Squad.

Although this Detroit boasts a population of less than 300, it has its share of stories. In sharing a few of these, I hope to give this rural town a voice about what life was like during the late 60s, 70s, and early 80s…

PART I
Never a Dull Moment

When I talk to people about the size of my hometown, many automatically assume my childhood must have been dull and non-eventful. That was not the case...

An Indoor Pool

When I look at a bottle of dish detergent, it sparks memories, oddly enough, of a time when I was only four years old. I really wanted a swimming pool at the time, but my father, being the frugal man he was, said, "We can't afford such a thing." Since there was no chance we could have a real pool behind our house, I came up with a plan and told my brother we could simply make one. Willy, who was only two years old at the time, always thought his big sister knew best, so he innocently went along with my idea.

One afternoon, our parents left my brother and me alone in the kitchen while they worked in the garden, only a few feet away from our house. This was a big mistake. I remember explaining my plan to Willy. I said, "All we have to do is stop up the kitchen sink, turn on the water, and watch." I knew that the water would eventually flow over onto the kitchen floor and create our much-wanted pool. Willy just nodded.

I pushed up a metal kitchen chair to the sink, climbed up onto the chair, and reached for the strainer. I maneuvered it just so. I turned on the faucet full blast. We waited in anticipation as the sink began to fill with water. After several minutes had passed, the water began to spill over onto the floor, little by little, until the small kitchen floor was completely saturated with water. As we sat down in the middle of our new pool, Willy and I agreed we needed something else to make the experience complete.

I remembered the dish detergent. It would be perfect. So I grabbed the bottle and began running around the kitchen, squirting the detergent all over the linoleum floor. This created not only bubbles, but also a slick surface that we could skate along. Now we had a pool and a skating rink! As the water continued to flow, the depth of our pool increased to about one-half of an inch. I remember sitting on the floor near the kitchen table and splashing both hands up and down in the water as the back door opened. Uh-oh.

It was our father, staring in disbelief. He had glanced over to the house and had seen what looked like water dripping from the back door. As he ran into the house, he glanced down to see two children happily splashing around amongst the water and bubbles. For a moment, he couldn't believe his eyes. He just stood there, as if in a trance, and surveyed the damage. Then, in his unemotional yet serious tone of voice, he asked, "Which one of you is responsible for this?"

Knowing what the consequences would be, I did the intelligent thing and simply pointed to my brother, who was quick to figure out that the best thing he could do was to repeat the gesture and point at me. I remember my daddy saying, "Well then, you'll both be punished." This was the last time I tried to create an indoor pool.

Slippery Slopes

One afternoon, when I was about five years of age, I noticed that my younger brother Willy had filled a galvanized metal tub with water and had placed his tiny wooden chair next to it. He had decided that afternoon to climb up onto the wooden chair and then jump feet first into the metal tub, which was about two feet tall and filled to the rim with water.

With mischief as my guide, I tiptoed to the kitchen and retrieved a bottle of dish detergent and then hid it behind my back as I watched Willy climb up time and time again onto this chair. When Willy went into the house to get a towel, I took advantage of the moment and ran over and squirted the clear liquid all over the seat of his wooden chair. After hiding the detergent behind some bushes, I sat on the grass and watched as my brother climbed back onto the chair. I knew that since the detergent was clear, it would go undetected.

I can still picture Willy standing up on the slippery chair, loosing his footing, and beginning to teeter like a trapeze artist in trouble on a tightrope. But his motions were much more exaggerated. One leg went high in the air. His arms outstretched in opposite directions. He then wobbled around like some sort of spinning top for a few seconds and fell headfirst into the tub of water. I remember rolling around on the ground, holding my stomach as I laughed, when Willy hit the water.

And then Daddy arrived on the scene.

Well…due to Daddy's philosophy about consequences for actions, let's just suffice it to say that I never squirted detergent in my brother's chair again.

Lived to Tell about It

Dishwashing liquid sure brings back some memories. I'll bet the dishwashing company could never have envisioned how many creative ways this substance could be used by children…

Once while visiting the with some of my friends on a hot summer day, Jessica suggested we squirt dishwashing liquid all over the nylon trampoline and place a water sprinkler underneath. This sounded like a good idea, at the time.

A few of us connected the water sprinkler to a hose, turned on the water, and watched as water shot five feet into the air, straight through the black nylon trampoline. It resembled Old Faithful. And once the dishwashing liquid was mixed with water from the sprinkler, the nylon surface of the trampoline became extremely slick, like a patch of ice.

While the thoughts of actually getting hurt never went through our minds, at least four of us climbed onto the trampoline, simultaneously, and started jumping high in the air. As our feet first made contact with this slick nylon surface, we'd slide across the entire diameter of the trampoline, which was about thirteen feet or so. A few times, we just kept on sliding and ended up on the ground or worst yet, stuck with one leg sandwiched between the metal coil springs and the other contorted in another direction. Since we were younger then, our muscles were obviously much more resilient, so we'd just climb back on the trampoline, jump high in the air, and then slide off again.

On one occasion, Jake decided he would climb on top of the roof of his house and then jump onto the wet trampoline. He was pretending to be Captain Marvel. If I remember correctly, he climbed onto the roof, waved Jessica's majorette baton, yelled, "Shazam!" and jumped fifteen feet or so onto the slippery trampoline. By some miracle and a little help from his guardian angel who was on call 24/7, Jake somehow landed on the trampoline, bounced onto the ground, and lived to tell about it.

If I'm not mistaken, I was the one who got hurt that day, nothing life threatening, just a few bruises after being caught between the metal coil springs. I had a reputation for being the clumsy one, who was usually afraid and therefore took very few risks, which reminds me of another story…

Horseback-riding

I was never the adventurous, risk-taking type. While Jake, Clint, and Jessica never batted an eye when it came to riding horses, motorcycles, and four-wheelers, I, on the other hand, often stood in the background analyzing all the risk factors, reminding them to be careful like some sort of overprotective mother. To me, just riding my bicycle was a major undertaking, so the thought of actually riding a horse was simply out of the question.

After a great deal of coercion on Jessica's part, I finally caved into the mounting peer pressure and agreed to ride one of her horses. Jessica promised me this particular horse, named Ginger, was extremely calm. In fact, I remember Jessica saying, "Tina, Ginger's as calm as they get. She's just about dead." Lori and Jessica agreed to ride along with me, so I tentatively hoisted my five-foot frame up onto the back of the horse and planted my feet in the stirrups. With Jessica seated at the front holding the reins and Lori in the middle, I was situated on the very back, holding onto Lori for dear life. Much to my surprise, the horseback-riding started out well as the three of us sat on Ginger's leather saddle. She trotted along the gravel path from Jessica's house over to Mr. Roy's and back as I looked around and took in the peaceful scenery of the farm. After thirty minutes or so, my heart rate was finally down to normal. I actually started to feel at ease with horseback-riding, when *it* happened.

Jake, Clint, and Willy spotted the three of us approaching on the horse and subsequently came up with a plan. The guys thought it would be a hoot to recreate a scene from a Civil War movie and charge toward the horse as they waved their Rebel flag. This, by the way, was no ordinary flag. It had dimensions of at least five feet by seven feet and was attached to a long metal pole. The moment the horse got a glimpse of the approaching flag, it reacted much like a bull would to a matador's cape and lifted its front legs off the ground, throwing the three of us backwards at a 90-degree angle.

I should have known better than to listen to Jessica.

I remember staring up at the sky and screaming. This, as I recall, didn't help matters. It only scared Ginger even more. She started to buck wildly, much like a mechanical bull. Although only a few seconds transpired, the whole scenario seemed to take place in slow motion. I remember seeing the horse's frightened eyes grow as big as saucers and the trees dance from side to side as I felt my grip on Lori slipping away. A few moments later, after being knocked around from one side to the other, I could hold on no longer and was thrown from the horse onto the rough gravel road, like some sort of inexperienced cowboy in his first rodeo.

As I found myself face down all sprawled out on the gravel road feeling much like Charlie Brown after Lucy predictably pulled away the football, I started to whisper to myself, "How in the world do I always manage to get myself in such predicaments?"

That was my last horseback-riding experience.

Chicken and Mud Pies

Grace - Suzie Collier

Oddly enough, I remember the first time I met Grace; we were both only four years of age....

Since we didn't grow up in a subdivision, interacting regularly with children from other households was somewhat of a challenge. To remedy this, Daddy always took it upon himself to take my brother and me over to the homes of other children for play dates, years before this was a common household term.

I remember my first play date with Grace, like it was yesterday. That afternoon, Daddy drove me over to the Alexanders' home. Like most families in Lamar County, he knew this family well; most importantly, he knew they had a daughter, who coincidentally was exactly my age. When we arrived at the Alexander residence, Virginia Mae suggested that Grace and I should play in the front yard. *Willie Mae Collier*

I remember hearing the screen door slam behind us as we walked outside. I also remember sitting down in the middle of some dirt and deciding to make some mud pies. To create these, I remember Grace telling me to pour cupfuls of water from a plastic container on top of the dirt. She then took a metal spoon and stirred the concoction. At some point, I remember the two of us plunging our tiny hands into the mixture and squishing the mud between our fingers. We then molded the wet dirt into small mounds and added some berries to the top of our mud pies.

The next thing I remember is a chicken moving in our direction, toward our treasured creation. Despite our attempts to ward off the approaching creature, the chicken won the battle and marched through the middle of our mud pies, leaving behind its own distinctive claw prints.

I suppose in many ways we, too, leave our own distinctive prints with people we encounter throughout our lives. With some people, we leave temporary impressions, like prints made along the seashore, which are soon washed away with the tide. With others, we leave lasting impressions, like prints formed in fresh cement. My friendship with Grace has been the latter; the impressions she has made on my life will always be a part of me.

Playhouses

No man is a failure who has friends.
~ Clarence, It's a Wonderful Life

Although I no longer live in the area where I grew up, I can picture it perfectly. In my mind, I visualize the dense woods behind our house, especially the set of trees just behind the vegetable garden. When I picture this area, I think about many things, but I often reflect on the playhouses we once built. I'm not sure if anything remains of our last playhouse. It has been years since I've walked that far back into those woods. As I envision the woods, the clock turns back to the year 1973 when I was ten, Jessica was nine, and Willy and Jake were both eight years old.

That year, we decided to build a playhouse. To locate some materials for this project, we plundered around our storage building. Somewhere we found a rectangular piece of corrugated scrap tin that was about six feet long and three feet wide; this served as our playhouse roof. We also found an old gas space heater with a cement back, which for some reason we thought we couldn't live without. And, tucked away in the corner of our storage building, we found my toy stove and refrigerator, which were both about three feet in height and were made of metal with painted knobs, burners, and handles. Mother helped with our project as well; she donated a pair of curtains, a few plastic bowls, some dented and slightly burned metal pans with miscellaneous lids, and several bent forks and spoons.

Once we'd collected our materials, Jessica and I needed help with moving these items to our chosen location. Willy and Jake were always recruited to do the heavy lifting. To Jessica and me, since they were boys, they should be the ones in charge of moving. Looking back at the fact that they were only eight years old at the time, this idea is quite humorous. But at the time, to two older, wiser and perhaps bossy sisters, it all seemed like the logical thing to do. Usually they were good sports about the whole thing and would agree to this task without too much persuasion on our part.

The moment we had everything moved to our new location, we would ask for the boys' help in nailing up the piece of tin which we would stretch between two trees, creating the perfect roof for our playhouse. After the roof was in place and the space heater was situated, our brothers were free to go about their business. The next step would be to create walls with the orange curtains by attaching these to the scrap tin or a nearby tree, and then we'd find the perfect spot for the metal refrigerator and stove.

When we finally had our nest made, we would spend the entire afternoon using our playhouse to role-play. On several occasions, we pretended to be hosting dinner parties where we entertained guests, the stuffed animals Mother had sown for us. As hosts, we created some very interesting recipes made of mud, garnished with leaves and small sticks. Of course, our imaginary guests were always impressed with our culinary skills.

After a few weeks of playhouse fun, we'd bore of our location and somehow coerce our brothers into finding a more suitable site. On average, we moved the playhouse at least three times a year. If you asked our brothers, they would likely say it was much more often than I remember. The cycle continued for a few years until one day we decided we were too old for the playhouse.

I doubt that anything still remains of the playhouses we built 30 years ago. Perhaps the next time I go back there, I will walk through those familiar woods and see what I come across. Even if the elements have eroded our furnishings, the memories remain as vivid as ever.

Jessica also had a playhouse. Her playhouse, though, was the envy of every elementary-age girl in the county. Unlike the one at my house that we had to construct out of scrap materials, her playhouse was a real house. It had an area of approximately 400 square feet, was made entirely of wood with a tin roof, and had a porch that stretched across the entire front. As you walked in, to the left you'd find a set of wooden bunk beds, nailed to the wall. Across from the beds was the kitchen, fully equipped with a real refrigerator, sink, and stove. And behind the kitchen area on the right wall was a wooden ladder, which led to the attic.

Once, for a few days, we even had electricity. Jessica's older brother Clint climbed up onto the roof of the playhouse and hooked up the electricity to an existing line, one intended for another building. The excitement lasted only briefly. Ken, Jessica's father, soon discovered our secret and understandably "pulled the plug" on our fun.

Jessica, Marie, Sherry, and I spent many hours engaged in role-playing in that playhouse. We practiced our culinary skills by making mud pies and other fabulous make-believe recipes. When Willy and Jake were around, they would often be sent on a mission to collect our cooking supplies; their job was to fill our canning jars with water and to bring back plenty of dirt for mud pies. However, many times we just couldn't seem to find our brothers. Mysteriously, they would disappear. Looking back, I can't say that I blame them for secretly running off to hide.

Since Jessica's playhouse had a yard, we spent many afternoons planting and watering a variety of flowers including old maids. Jessica even concocted a fountain from an old tin pan in which she would throw in leaves and other decorations that would float. Willy and Jake were somehow recruited to fill this pan on a regular basis.

Jake once asked, "Why in the world does that pan needed to be filled so often?"

Jessica spouted off something about evaporation to sound intelligent, but secretly she knew the pan had a few small holes in it.

Although we loved working on the curb appeal of the playhouse, one of our favorite things was to climb up into the attic, which was only about three feet high. After we climbed the wooden ladder to the top, we had to carefully bend over as we walked around the confined space. The playhouse's attic had one window, about twelve inches in width. Here, we spent many afternoons looking out that particular window in hopes that we could somehow spy on people. Actually from this vantage point, we could see few people, so we often just used our imagination and made up different scenarios.

Jessica's childhood playhouse no longer stands. Over time, the wooden structure suffered from the elements of nature and was torn down. Although it's no longer visible, it, too, resides in my memory just as it was years ago.

Swimming Holes

There are moments when I see a certain building or grove of trees and almost feel like I'm traveling back in time, reliving some moment from my past, just as I experienced it all twenty or thirty years ago. This happened to me recently, when I drove by the old homeplace where I'd grown up. As I passed over the creek that flowed near our childhood home, some memories flashed through my mind that made me feel like I was reliving it all over again…

This summer afternoon in 1972 started out like many others in the rural south. Since the heat index was well over 100 degrees and the humidity registered in at around 90 percent, we opted to cool down by spending some time playing in the creek's culvert that was located about fifty yards from our house. Situated in the middle of our creek, the metal corrugated culvert was about fifteen feet in length and had a diameter of ten feet or so and contained water that normally was only deep enough to splash around our ankles.

That day, Jake, Jessica, Willy, and I decided to build a dam inside the creek's culvert to create some deeper water, so we could actually do some swimming. Our plan was to simply build a retaining wall, using some old scrap boards, along one opening of the culvert so a pool of rising water could form.

For about thirty minutes or so, the makeshift wall we'd created held back the creek's water, so water did slowly start to rise. What usually only covered our ankles was now waist deep. Excited by our discovery and ingenuity, we started to swim around inside the culvert like it was some sort of wading pool. Then, without warning, we heard something that sounded like roaring thunder as it echoed within the confines of the metal culvert.

The laws of physics held true that day. The force of the creek's water made the makeshift dam suddenly collapse. Water that had been contained inside the culvert spilled forth into the other side of the creek with an immense amount of energy, carrying along with it many of our belongings. My pink rubber ball, we'd played with inside the culvert, went downstream with the rest of the wreckage. Briefly, we entertained the thought of swimming out to the middle of the creek to retrieve the ball, but by this time it had floated into the deep water over by the creek bank where we suspected water moccasins might be. Even Jessica wasn't brave enough to attempt this one. And so we watched, as the pink ball and several of our belongings slowly drifted downstream.

To my knowledge, this is the only "tragedy" we experienced as we swam in numerous creeks. The other memories I have are pleasant ones such as swinging freely from a rope tied to a nearby oak tree into a creek we called the Johnson Hole, wading around in the icy waters of Sipsey Creek, and watching Jessica do cartwheels and ride her bike along the narrow ten-inch bridge rails that covered Dry Creek over near Clint's house. There was never a dull moment in Detroit, Alabama.

Games Children Play

When we were young, we often played Chase. I despised this game, but my one vote invariably lost out to the rest of the group, so I usually went along with this idea and tried to make the best of it.

One Sunday afternoon, Clint and Michael, who were both five years older than any member of our team, declared they'd be one team; the rest of us would be the other. I had an eerie premonition about this particular game. I did the math in my head. I knew the odds of my team actually winning were next to zero, since Clint was 6'6" at the time and as solid as steel. I didn't think we had a chance. My teammates, though, naively thought otherwise.

Our team consisted of five members: Willy, Jake, Jessica, Lori, and me. Since Clint and Michael were both sixteen years old at the time, we convinced them to give us a running start. They yelled, "Run!" We scurried about as fast as our little legs would carry us.

After five minutes or so had passed, we somehow made it over to one of Ken's barns. Here, we tried to hide behind some farm equipment and then tried to weave in and out, like we'd seen cops do on television, as we made our way around to the corner of the barn. This system worked for a little while, about fifteen minutes or so.

Somehow, like snakes in the grass, Michael and Clint slithered up behind us, while we were perched behind a tractor. When my teammates and I caught a glimpse of the two guys, we started to sprint. I tried my best, but I was never that athletic. With my small frame, my legs were just too short to match the strides of Clint. As I ran and yelled for my teammates to wait on me, I watched in dismay as my team members hurdled the wooden fence into safety. I was left behind. I was now a POW.

Much to my despair, Clint thought the game should be as realistic as possible, so he wasted no time and tied me up with the yellow rope his father used with cattle. Moments later, after he'd secured my hands and feet, Clint decided he would hang me upside down from one of the nearby oak trees.

My teammates, realizing that I'd been captured, tried some rescue attempts (or so they say) while I dangled for a few minutes upside down, staring down at the gravel road. Somehow during the time Clint was preoccupied with tying me up, my friends did manage to arrive back at the Cash residence and informed Laura about my predicament. As soon as she heard about my capture, she headed out the door. I can still picture Laura, walking with her fists clenched at her side, like an angry sergeant, over in my direction.

"Clinton Wesley Cash, untie Tina right this second!"

"But mama, it's only a game."

"I'm going to make you think game if you don't untie her right this second!"

And so, I have Laura to thank for coming to my rescue. It's anyone's guess how long Clint would have allowed me to dangle like that, upside down, bobbing around like someone dangling from a bungee cord.

This, by the way, was the last time I played this game.

In Disguise

Jessica was a character. Through the years, I've often referred to Jessica as Lucy and to myself as Ethel. Like Lucille Ball, Jessica could concoct some of the funniest scenarios.

One Sunday afternoon when we were around eleven years of age, Jessica decided we needed some excitement in the town of Detroit, so she thought it would be funny to impersonate someone. Jessica convinced me that she could just borrow some of her mother's clothes and pose as a middle-aged woman.

Since Jessica's mother was over at Mrs. Maggie's, we tiptoed over to her closet, while Ken dozed a few yards away in his favorite recliner. After examining several outfits in Laura's closet, Jessica selected a double-knit dress, a pair of beige pantyhose, and some shiny black patent Sunday dress shoes. She also managed to find a pair of sunglasses as well as a brunette wig with loose wavy curls, found tucked away in her mom's hatbox. Once she dressed herself with the hose, black high heels, peach-colored knit dress, dark sunglasses, and brunette wig, Jessica looked like a chic middle-aged woman. She was now ready for her début.

Jessica instructed me to just hang out in the kitchen with her younger brother Jake while she went around to the front door. From our vantage point in the kitchen, we were able to witness the entire production. While Ken took a Sunday afternoon nap in his recliner, Jessica wobbled around in her high heels to the front of the house and rang the doorbell, the sound of which awoke Ken from his slumber and caused him to spring from the recliner. When Ken opened the front door, he was met by a petite brunette, dressed in her Sunday best, standing on the doorstep. The brunette whispered with a sweet Southern accent, "Sir, I'm afraid I've accidentally wrecked my car and really need some assistance."

"Why yes ma'am, I'll be glad to help you. Just let me go get my jacket."

After walking across the room and retrieving his jacket from the coat rack, Ken approached the door once more, extending his arms through the jacket's sleeves. As he adjusted his jacket collar, he stared at the young woman and started to detect something oddly familiar. And then the answer came to him. When the young brunette smiled, she flashed a set of braces. In the mere blink of an eye, her cover was blown.

Realizing who she was at that instant, Ken simply chuckled, "Oh, Jessica, get in this house, you silly thing." Jake and I laughed as tears rolled down our faces. Ken rarely fell for anything, and Jessica had almost gotten the best of him. Ken later told us if Jessica had not smiled that day, he would have probably fallen for her little stunt…hook, line, and sinker.

Look-a-Likes

To be honest, Jessica wasn't the only one that disguised herself as someone else. Grace and I also did this one summer night.

The plan was Grace's and involved posing as her younger sister Kathryn. I was to pretend to be Anna, Kathryn's best friend. Grace and Kathryn looked remarkably similar; many said they could pass for identical twins, even though Grace was five years older. Anna and I were both petite and brunette, so from a distance we probably resembled each other…somewhat. Grace decided that we should ride around the small town of Hamilton and pose as Kathryn and Anna.

This particular night we drove around the winding path in Hamilton. Each small town had its own path that teenagers drove around each weekend. Hamilton's path started out at the Sonic, went straight downtown, turned right, and then looped around near the Hardee's fast-food restaurant. Grace and I had made it over to the Hardee's when some younger guys (Kathryn and Anna's age) motioned for us to pull over.

Grace took one look at me, smirked, and said, "Remember, you're Anna."

We pulled up beside the guys. They rolled down their car window, leaned over in our direction, and asked us our names.

Grace and I whispered, "Anna Christopher and Kathryn Alexander" using our sweetest Southern accents.

The guys replied, "Oh, yeah. We've heard about you."

Grace didn't miss a beat. "So, what have you heard?"

"Well, we've heard you're from Detroit, that you're really nice girls, and that you've dated some guys from Hamilton."

Knowing to whom they were referring, Grace asked, "So, are you friends with these guys?"

"No. Not really, we just know them from our high school, that's all."

As the conversation progressed, the guys, thinking that we were really Anna and Kathryn, asked us for our phone numbers. After a few minutes had transpired, Grace and I looked at each other with mischievous grins and gave them the phone numbers of Anna and Kathryn.

After all, showing hospitality is a sign of a true Southern lady.

19

Shear Effects

One Sunday afternoon, Jessica and I started flipping through magazines, looking for the latest in trendy hairstyles. Jessica had the bright idea that I should, for some unknown reason, dye my hair blonde even though my hair was a rather dark brunette shade. Unfortunately, on this afternoon, I was easily coerced into this. Instead of making plans to purchase a bottle of semi-permanent hair color, Jessica insisted she had a better idea.

I should have known better.

Jessica said, "Bend over and put your hair in the sink."

Without thinking, I did. Jessica then poured the contents of an entire bottle of bleach onto my hair.

I asked, "Are you sure you know what you're doing?"

"Of course I do," replied Jessica.

Well, she didn't.

Once we washed and dried my hair, one could only imagine the results.

I had skunk hair.

Multi-colored with random streaks of blonde, brown, and some color that resembled a dirty carrot pulled right out of the ground, my hair was a sight.

As I looked into the mirror, I screamed, "How can we fix this?"

Jessica replied, "Let's use some more bleach, to even things out."

Since we had used the last drop of her mom's only bottle, this was no longer an option. I panicked and thought maybe I could wash it all out. After scrubbing my hair five times with some green shampoo, I realized that washing was having little to no effect. With evening church services quickly approaching, I had to come up with another plan to camouflage my hair. In desperation, I decided to just wear my hair in a ponytail in hopes that no one would notice.

As you can imagine, all forty or so members of Detroit First Baptist could not help but notice as I made my entrance into the small sanctuary. I can still picture the second glances and shrugged shoulders of the ladies in our church. I vowed to never listen to Jessica's hair advice again. Of course, I sometimes have been known to have a short memory…

A few months after the infamous bleaching incident, Jessica spent the night with me as we made plans to go with my family on a shopping trip to Tupelo. That night, Jessica and I started talking about how Mary had such wonderful hair. She had this short sassy style that curled in just the right places and was the envy of every teenage girl at Sulligent High. This conversation brought about another brilliant idea. Jessica decided that since my hair was somewhat wavy, she could style it just perfectly, and I'd end up with a hairstyle that looked exactly like Mary's. I bought into this wholeheartedly and became excited about the possibility of having hair just like Mary's.

To accomplish this look, Jessica said, "I'm going to roll your hair on these pink sponge rollers while it's still wet." With this, she added another element; she twisted my wet hair in a rope-like fashion and then curled it around the pink rollers. Once again, this seemed logical, even though the directions on the sponge roller bag clearly stated to use with hair that was completely dry.

Later I would learn that directions are there for a reason. The next morning the moment arrived when we could take down my hair and admire my new coif. After all this anticipation, I was excited to show off my new hairstyle as we shopped in Tupelo; I just knew I'd be the talk of the town. Well, this part was correct. When I took out the rollers, combed through my hair and stared into the mirror, I saw someone who resembled Medusa. To make matters worse, Daddy started calling for us to get into the car.

Jessica took one look at me and tried to hold back her laughter as she said, "It doesn't look *that* bad."

I knew better. I had snake hair.

So…to make the best of the situation, I tried the ponytail remedy, but my bangs stuck out in every direction with no rhyme or reason. I was a victim once more…

Honestly though, Jessica bought in to some of my wonderful ideas as well. When Jessica was in the third grade, we decided she needed some bangs. Somehow I convinced Jessica, although I was only in the fourth grade, I knew how to cut hair. I remember going down to the basement and getting a pair of Laura's favorite sewing scissors, made of stainless steel with orange plastic handles. After combing out Jessica's long blonde hair, I took the scissors and started cutting. This, by the way, was my first hair trimming experience. I believe I neglected to tell Jessica this fact.

When I made the first cut, Jessica yelled, "I think that's too short! Let me see a mirror."

She looked in the mirror and realized that the part I cut left her with bangs about one inch from her scalp. Realizing this, she made me stop. So there she sat with about a two-inch section that was shorter than the rest of her hair. This gap was quite noticeable; although I tried to convince her otherwise. I tried to persuade her into letting me cut a little bit more to even it all out, but I suppose she'd somehow lost all confidence in my cutting abilities. We still have some evidence of this scenario. One of her elementary school photos will forever tell this story.

In later years, I convinced Jessica that she should straighten her hair so she would resemble Marcia Brady. At this point in time, most young teenagers only dreamed of looking like Marcia with her long straight style. We somehow purchased a straightening kit and started to work on Jessica's hair one Sunday afternoon. I remember trying to follow the directions on the box. Perhaps I left it on too long; this part I don't remember. The part I do remember is when we were finished and decided to blow dry Jessica's hair to see how wonderful her newly straightened style would be. Well, let's just say that she did not look like Marcia Brady. The hair concoction worked a little too well. It took all of the body out of my friend's hair, leaving it straight and as lifeless as a wooden board.

I tried to console her. "It doesn't look that bad." Secretly, I wanted to laugh out loud. "Let's just go across the street and ask your grandparents if they notice anything different."

Jessica just nodded.

We walked across the street and found Mr. Roy and Mrs. Belle sitting on the front porch drinking some sweet tea. As soon as Mr. Roy got a good look at Jessica he said, "Sugar, what's wrong with your hair? It's sticking to your head like a drowned rat."

You could always count on Mr. Roy and Mrs. Belle to shoot straight with you.

Well I almost fell off the porch laughing. I'd held it in all the way from Jessica's house and could contain it no longer. It was one of those times when I wasn't supposed to laugh, which, of course, only made matters worse.

As Jessica explained what had happened, I tried to come up with a plan to remedy the situation. I convinced Jessica that we could simply wash out the straightening solution. She concurred that this was at least worth a try so we went back to her house and washed and dried her hair over and over again. But there was a problem. Time was running out. We had to get ready for our evening church service at Detroit First Baptist, which started promptly at five-thirty. After the seventh or so washing, Jessica dried and attempted to style her newly straightened hair. Washing her hair did seem to help a little (at least that's what I kept telling her).

On the way to church, I remember her mother's quizzical look and comment, "Young lady, what in the world have you done to your hair?"

As we entered the church, several people stared at Jessica's new hairstyle as if they were thinking, "Did she put oil on her head?" As people started to whisper, several of the elderly ladies turned their heads to get a better view of Jessica's new slick style and then shrugged their shoulders. Jessica, too, had made an impression...

A Dangling Speaker and a Speedy Exit

At the age of thirteen, one cannot legally drive in Alabama, so we were often dependent on others for transportation. Knowing this, one evening after our church services, Jessica, Lori, and I convinced Jessica's mother to take us to the drive-in theatre located in nearby Guin to see a movie. We assured Laura the movie was appropriate for our age group; therefore, Jessica's mom agreed to take us. My brother Willy and Jessica's brother Jake, who were both eleven years of age at the time, wanted to tag along as well. So, one Sunday night, following one of our church services, we all piled into Laura's green Impala. As I remember it, Willy and Jake sat in the front next to Laura while we girls situated ourselves in the roomy backseat.

When we arrived at the Gu-Win Drive-In, Laura carefully situated the speaker just so on the driver's window as we settled down to watch the movie with our butter-flavored tubs of popcorn and some 32-ounce fountain drinks. At first, the movie was uneventful and a tired Laura slowly drifted off to sleep. About twenty minutes after Laura had fallen asleep, a love scene appeared on the screen, which caused Jessica, Lori, and me to let out some girlish giggles. Understandably, the giggling from the backseat caused Laura to wake up. As she awoke from her slumber, Laura glanced at the movie screen and quickly assessed the situation. She immediately realized what was making us giggle and made an executive decision.

"We're not watching this filth!"

Faster than a speeding bullet, Laura threw the speaker out the car window, leaving it to dangle around the metal pole, and then proceeded to crank the Impala. She turned the headlights on high beam. Before we knew what had happened, we were bouncing down the middle of the terraces with our blinding headlights bumping along the way like some sort of Sherman tank speeding along rocky terrain. Instead of taking the regular winding path designed for departure, Laura created a new one, right down the middle of the outdoor theatre's parking lot. As car horns began to blow, we sank down deep into the floorboard of the car, hoping and praying no one we knew would recognize any of us.

For the entire duration of the trip home, Laura commented on how inappropriate the content of the movie was; we were inundated with the "I'm disappointed in you" talk. This was the ultimate torture; we would rather just receive a spanking any day, when given the choice. Although the ride home was only about sixteen miles, it seemed like an eternity. Thoughts raced through our minds. Was 'the talk' the only punishment or was there more to come? I began to envision my father saying his infamous quote, "You ought to be ashamed."

Once we arrived back at the Cash residence, Ken met us in the kitchen and eagerly asked, "So...how was the movie?"

An aggravated Laura responded, "It wasn't fit for our dog Friskie to watch!"

Laura offered to drive my brother and me home. After what had transpired, we really would have preferred to just walk the five-mile distance. Knowing that this wasn't a real option at this hour, we nodded and tentatively climbed back into the Impala. There was a deadly silence that hung in the air like a thick fog as Laura drove. For the duration of the trip, we made a special effort to avoid conversation and to especially avoid any possible eye contact with Laura. We stared intently at the floorboard of the car and occasionally glanced out the window.

When Laura pulled up into our driveway, we thanked her for bringing us home as we carefully avoided her eyes and bolted for our front door, praying the whole time that she would not share our movie experience with Daddy.

And to my knowledge, she never said a word to Daddy. I suppose she felt we'd suffered enough.

On a Hot Tin Roof

Before the days of SPF sunscreen and our awareness of the sun's damaging effects, many afternoons were spent basking in the sun's rays in Jessica's back-yard. Jessica was a sun-bathing connoisseur. She seemed to have all the answers when it came to acquiring the perfect tan. Jessica also put a great deal of thought into making the sun bathing experience more bearable by hooking up a nearby water sprinkler and plugging in an oscillating fan as well as providing us with a radio tuned to our favorite station and a few tasty snacks in a handy nearby fridge.

One day, a sunbathing invention came along that caught Jessica's eye. This invention, a silver blanket, resembled a large piece of aluminum foil and reflected the sun's rays, thus enabling those who used it to obtain a dark even tan in just a fraction of the time. This was just what Jessica thought we needed. Since neither Jessica nor I owned this innovative contraption, she had an ingenious idea to obtain the same effect.

I should have known better.

Of course, without thinking, I listened to my friend's idea and followed her lead. At the time, the idea seemed quite plausible, even quite logical. Her idea was to just replicate the contraption by making use of the tin roof on top of one of her father's barns. The roof looked just like the reflecting blanket. Jessica and I agreed it would be perfect. So, one very hot and humid afternoon in August, we packed our bags complete with a radio, some beach towels, a bottle of baby oil, and a few snacks as we set off to our new sun bed location. Once we climbed on top of the barn's roof, we adjusted our beach towels and tuned in to our favorite radio station. Next, we smothered ourselves in baby oil and settled down to soak up the warm sun's rays.

Warm is perhaps an understatement. This was an afternoon in August, in the state of Alabama, when the humidity was just under 100 percent. In record time, say seven minutes or so, I was quite miserable. Yes, the barn's roof did reflect the August rays quite well…too well for me. I was convinced the roof's temperature was over 125 degrees Fahrenheit, so I began to literally beg Jessica to scrap the plan and find a more suitable location. Of course, to my misfortune, Jessica's tolerance for heat was much higher than mine.

Jessica wiped the sweat off of her forehead and said, "If you don't think about the heat, it won't bother you."

I tried her advice. She was wrong.

After a few more minutes, I replied, "I can't take this another minute!" So, I stood up, gathered my belongings and attempted to walk down the incline of the barn's tin roof.

Not surprisingly, like many of the ideas in the past, Jessica's plan was not well thought through. The problem was I had done a very good job applying baby oil. When I stood up, the soles of my rubber flip-flops were covered with this slick substance. With a sloping roof, the smooth surface of tin, and nothing to hold on to, I immediately started to ski off the top of the barn like someone in the Winter Olympics. I still remember the horrified look on Jessica's face as I turned to her and yelled.

During those few seconds as I watched the ground grow closer and closer, I remember thinking about how many bones I would break and how embarrassed I would be to explain to people how I had broken them. As I began to slide off the barn's roof, my life flashed before my eyes like someone had pressed fast forward on the VCR.

Luckily for me, the barn's roof was only about eight feet or so off the ground and hay was scattered all around its perimeter; therefore, my landing, although abrupt, was cushioned. So thanks to a few bales of hay, I survived my first skiing experience without a broken bone or even a bruise.

As soon as I was able to get back on my feet again, I yelled in Jessica's direction. "I'm okay! I landed in some of your daddy's hay. Please come down off the roof."

Deciding that she should try to descend as well, Jessica attempted to stand up but soon discovered that she, too, had liberally applied the baby oil. Without any ski poles of her own, Jessica slid down the tin ramp in a matter of seconds. Like mine, Jessica's guardian angel must have also been on call; she landed among the hay bales and walked away from the accident without so much as a scratch. Since that day, neither of us has ventured on top of a barn's roof.

A Dummy on Dry Creek Road

One hot muggy summer night, when the humidity was hovering just under 100 percent, my brother and his two friends, Jake and Phillip, were having a campout in the woods about a half-mile or so from Jake's house. Early that evening, the guys decided the town needed a little entertainment, so they concocted what at the time seemed to be an ingenious idea. They took a pair of worn out overalls and an old white shirt, stuffed the clothing with hay, added some muddy brogans, and in no time created a dummy. Since they could not figure out a way to attach a head to their dummy, they simply decided he would go without. When nightfall approached, they carefully placed the dummy in a ditch, threw tomatoes at him, and hid in a nearby location to watch the reaction of passing motorists.

In this remote area, cars passed, on average, every half-hour or so. Since the guys were fully aware of the odds of a car actually traveling down this path, they found a hiding spot, made themselves comfortable in the soybean patch, and waited patiently. Twenty minutes later, they spotted the first car approaching. Much to their dismay, the first car sped by, totally oblivious to the dummy. The guys decided to pull him out to the road so that his brown farm boots were barely touching the edge of the blacktop and his upper body was positioned in the ditch then settled back to wait patiently for the next motorist. Surprisingly, another car came down the road just fifteen minutes later, but continued on, without the slightest loss in acceleration.

Jake, Willy, and Phillip, now exasperated by the two motorists, decided to pull the dummy further out onto the highway. After what seemed like an eternity, another automobile approached, reduced its speed, and then proceeded to travel down the road. Before the guys could move, they noticed the driver hit the brakes, threw the car into reverse, and slowly started to back up, curving in a snake-like fashion, finally coming to a stop, just inches from the dummy.

Willy, Jake, and Phillip peeked around from behind their hiding place and saw the back of the car's taillights and a woman slowly emerging from the car. The woman tentatively tiptoed over to the dummy, stopped to inspect it from several feet way, and then started screaming and waving her outstretched arms.

"Oh Lordy! It's my brother! He walks these roads all the time!"

As she continued to fling her arms frantically in the air, the woman sprinted to her car and sped away like someone in the Daytona 500.

Little did they know that the fiasco was just beginning.

While they rolled around on the ground holding their stomachs as they laughed, the woman drove to the nearest house, which coincidentally happened to be Jake's. She sped into the gravel driveway causing small pebbles to fly six feet or so in the air. The moment the car came to a stop she bounded from the vehicle and started to pound on the front door.

Ken, Jake's father, went to answer the door and listened carefully as the lady frantically told him how she'd found her brother lying in a nearby ditch. Unaware of the guys' prank, Ken promptly did the responsible thing and called the town's Rescue Squad as well as the county's sheriff.

To fully picture and appreciate this story, one must understand the terrain of this area. Detroit is located in northwest Alabama, only a few miles from Mississippi; therefore the land is flat. Consequently, people can see for miles. As Willy, Jake, and Phillip sat around their campfire feeling rather smug, they spotted an array of lights approaching in the distance as thoughts raced through their minds.

Could that be an ambulance? Could the other one be a police car? Are they coming in this direction?

As they began to do the math and put two and two together, lumps formed in their throats. Maybe the prank wasn't such a good idea after all. As the emergency vehicles arrived, the guys realized the severity of the prank, panicked, and much like Adam and Eve in the Garden of Eden, ran to hide.

In this town of less than three hundred people, word travels faster than the speed of light. In seconds, not only was an ambulance on the scene, but most of the townspeople as well. Interestingly enough, three of the town's teenagers were missing. As everyone gathered around the crime scene, Ken was the first to notice who was missing. He quietly leaned over to his wife Laura and whispered in her ear.

"Are you thinking what I'm thinking?"

A moment later, Ken climbed into his white truck to apprehend the suspects.

After deciding to go back to the campsite, the teenagers began to see another set of lights slowly approaching in the distance. They could make out the outline of the vehicle as it topped the hill. *Uh-oh.*

As the headlights approached over the small field, their lives flashed before their eyes. They knew they had to come up with a plan. In an effort to avoid looking guilty, Jake said, "Don't look at him. Just stare at the campfire."

When the truck came to a stop, an ominous figure emerged. The figure was that of a farmer with a 6'4" intimidating frame, who had a strong resemblance to Sheriff Taylor from Mayberry. At that moment, my brother got a glimpse of Ken's face and noticed that one of his pupils was rather dilated. This only happened occasionally and was a sure sign that Ken was not a happy camper. Ken sauntered over to the guys.

"Are you boys the ones responsible for all this excitement we've had tonight?"

After a moment of silence, Jake stared at the fire and simply replied, "What excitement?"

Ken was not amused. "I'm only going to ask you boys one more time. Are you responsible for all this commotion?"

Jake chuckled, in a desperate attempt to lighten the mood, and said, "Daddy, isn't it kind of funny?"

Ken responded, "Boys, the party is over. Y'all put out that fire and hop in the back of the truck. You'll be spending the night in the basement. Y'all have caused enough excitement for one night."

Knowing better than to even think about arguing with Ken, the guys slowly meandered over to the campfire, with their heads hung low, and took their time pouring out all their three-liter drinks over the fire. The fire extinguished, they tentatively climbed in the back of the pickup truck. The guys recalled that the ride to the house, although just less than a half mile, seemed to take forever and a day.

When the guys arrived at the house, Jake's mother met them at the door. Laura took one look at them and said, "I'm disappointed in you all. You boys know better than to act like that. You've gotten the whole town in a tizzy."

Later, the guys said they remembered Laura slightly chuckling about the whole commotion. Although Ken refused to smile that night, in later years, he has been known to laugh when he reflects on all the commotion created by the headless dummy placed on Dry Creek Road.

Life on the Farm

After spending all day in the scorching August sun that had beaten down relentlessly on their backs, the guys felt relieved as they gazed up at the neatly stacked hay bales that filled the back of Ken's pickup. This was the last load. They had somehow survived the hot muggy day, although at times, they were not sure they would. Since the crack of dawn, they had been in the hay fields wrestling with rectangular shaped bales of hay that had to be thrown onto trucks and then unloaded at the barn. Now it was finally quitting time.

Mr. Roy, Jake's grandfather, decided to drive one of the pickup trucks which was loaded down with fifty-pound hay bales. Willy and Jake situated themselves on top of the freshly stacked bales. As they brushed a few strands of hay from their hair and wiped sweat mixed with caked-on dirt from their faces, they leaned back onto the hay bales and enjoyed the warm breeze created by the moving truck. After a mile or so, they approached a rather steep hill. Mr. Roy glanced back at the rearview mirror and for some unknown reason started to slow down. Willy and Jake took one look at each other and exchanged worried glances. They realized that the slightest loss in acceleration would cause the entire load of hay to come tumbling down. So the guys leaned up against the truck's rear window, pounded on top of the truck with their fists and yelled in unison, "Go! Go!"

Mr. Roy, who couldn't hear worth a lick, thought they said, "Whoa! Whoa!"

Mr. Roy then slammed on the brakes about the moment the truck was perched at a 45-degree angle. With a little hesitation, most of the hay bales along with the guys tumbled out onto the hard ground, like pouring cereal from a box.

Mr. Roy glanced back at the rearview mirror and caught a glimpse of the guys as well as the hay all sprawled out along the ground. He put on the emergency brake and climbed out of the truck. Mr. Roy stared at the scattered hay bales that looked like they'd just been tossed around by a tornado. Then he commenced to yelling.

"Good night alive! Can't you two boys stack hay no better than that?"

Willy and Jake sat up and brushed the strands of hay from their shirts, which were saturated with dirt and sweat.

"We were just trying to tell you to go on."

Mr. Roy, took out his cotton handkerchief, wiped the sweat from his brow, and shook his head. "Well, stop all that hollering! Look at what a mess you two made."

The Humidity in the South Can Play Tricks on You

The heat in the south can do some pretty strange things to you. Some folks blame the humidity. Regardless, one or both of these elements seemed to have an adverse effect on my brother Willy and friend Jake on more than one occasion...

After pulling weeds in the hundred-acre soybean patch in the heat of a late July day, Willy and Jake decided to pretend they were weeds; they thought it would be a hoot to duck down low behind the densely planted soybean plants and then take off running whenever a car passed. They could just picture people driving by, taking in the peaceful scenery of the fields, and then catching a glimpse of walking weeds.

At this point, I'm not sure if the guys were delirious or dehydrated or just plain exhausted, but they decided to camouflage themselves as plants by simply securing weeds all over their caps and shirts. As cars approached, they started sprinting behind the soybeans with weeds attached to their caps and shoulders.

I have no idea what the motorists thought. As far as I know, this incident, unlike previous ones, never made it to the local authorities.

If you are ever in Detroit, Alabama, and notice soybean plants moving around, don't despair; it's probably just the humidity playing tricks on you.

Blowtorches, Hammers, and Warm Bottles

Mr. Matthews served as Willy and Jake's Ag teacher during their high school years. He was a kind man who believed that his adolescent students were intrinsically motivated to be productive with their time and could stay on task, with or without his constant intervention. In other words, Mr. Matthews believed his students could regulate their own behavior. And if they abused this privilege, they were required to leave the woodworking area and go to the adjoining classroom to take notes. Since Mr. Matthews trusted his students (for the most part), they were given ample opportunities to work independently on a variety of projects.

This was a big mistake.

One day, Mr. Matthews assigned a project to Willy and Jake. He had noticed that a few windowpanes in the Ag building were cracked and therefore needed to be replaced. For some reason, he entrusted Willy and Jake with this job.

As Mr. Matthews handed the fifteen-year old guys a couple of hammers, he gave them explicit instructions. "Boys, I need you to take these hammers and break out them cracked windows."

Willy and Jake took one look at each other. Jake smiled like a child in a candy store. Then, they repeated in unison, "Yes, sir!"

The teenage guys, understandably, were very enthusiastic about this project. As soon as Mr. Matthews left the room, they spun around the room, like bees buzzing around a hive, moving from window to window, tapping on the glass with their hammers, and knocking out windowpanes.

Mr. Matthews had instructed them to only knock out the windowpanes that were cracked. Following orders, they did knock out only the cracked windows, but as they flew around the room with hammers in their hands, more windows mysteriously developed cracks. As they buzzed around the room, enthusiastically knocking out windowpanes, Mr. Matthews burst through the swinging door. He looked around and surveyed the floor, covered with shards of glass.

"Dad blame it! What in the world are you two doing?"

"We are breaking out the cracked panes…Sir."

"I know you two got more sense than that!" Mr. Matthews said. "Hand me them hammers."

Moments later, they were instructed to go to the adjoining classroom and take notes.

Months after the infamous windowpane project, Willy and Jake climbed up to the attic, walked around, and noticed a small hole about three inches or so in diameter. Interestingly enough, this hole was positioned right above the table saw.

This gave them an idea.

As Mr. Matthews walked over to the table saw to demonstrate some techniques for cutting, Willy and Jake, who had a perfect view of the top of their teacher's head, decided to drop wood chips from the ceiling. As soon as the first wood chip hit the top of his head, Mr. Matthews started yelling at the other boys in the class, who were innocently observing him. This continued for quite some time until their teacher put two and two together and cocked his head toward the ceiling.

"Jake and Willy…get down here right this minute!"

After receiving a paddling for their little wood chip prank, they were soon instructed to go to the adjoining classroom, take their places in their wooden desks, get out their notebooks, and take plenty of notes.

A few months later, Willy and Jake were walking around the attic during Ag class and noticed a mop. They decided it would be a hoot to place the mop handle through the hole in the ceiling and tap students on the head. After lowering the mop, they would quickly tap someone on the head, pull it up through the opening, and chuckle as they watched people turn their heads back and forth to determine who had hit them. This worked well for about fifteen minutes or so until their teacher walked in unannounced, looked up at the ceiling, and witnessed a mop handle bobbing up and down.

"Get down here Jake and Willy!"

The mop handle suddenly stopped in mid-air.

Weeks later, the National Guard donated a Jeep to the agricultural department. The organization's intent was to donate a vehicle to the Ag class so the guys could learn auto mechanics from a hands-on approach. The teenage boys, though, had a different idea. After the Jeep was delivered to campus, the guys in the agricultural class looked at each other with mischievous grins and came up with a plan.

The plan involved blowtorches.

Mr. Matthews had recently taught them how to work with blowtorches. Someone suggested they use this equipment on the Jeep. So…whenever they had some down time, the guys would walk over to the Jeep with their tools, like they were working alongside an assembly line in an automotive plant. They took to this project wholeheartedly. Each day they would work on the Jeep and distort its appearance a little more. By the end of the semester, the jeep appeared as if it had been used throughout World War II; all that was left of the original Jeep was a measly frame that resembled something like a child's go-cart.

Another incident involved a bottle of all-purpose cleaner. This bottle of cleaner (which happened to have a yellow hue) was something Mr. Matthews used to clean the basin of the sink after he washed his hands. One of the guys examined the bottle and concocted an idea. He filled it with a human waste product, replaced the bottle's cap, and placed the bottle back on the sink. The guys then hid in the attic and peeked out through the small hole to witness Mr. Matthew's reaction.

After a few minutes, Mr. Matthews walked up to the sink, washed his hands, and then proceeded to pour the contents from the bottle all over the basin of the sink. As he began to wipe the liquid around the sink, he made some rather keen observations.

"What's wrong with this stuff? It won't suds." As he scrubbed even harder, he realized what it was and yelled, "I bet I know what this is. The bottle's still warm!"

They watched as Mr. Matthews threw the bottle into the wastebasket and burst through the swinging doors like Festus leaving a saloon on the set of *Gunsmoke* and yelled, "Boys, get in your desks right this minute! We're going to have class!"

◆   ◆   ◆

Years later, the Ag building was torn down. This should come as no surprise.

Domestically Challenged

While Willy and Jake enrolled in Ag classes at Sulligent High, Grace, Jessica, Kathryn, Anna, and I enrolled in Home Economics. Mrs. Stanford, our Home Economics teacher, was keenly observant and involved in every assignment. In other words, she had what educators call "with-it-ness." There was never any downtime in her class. Regardless of whether we were whipping up things from scratch in our kitchen area or creating outfits at our assigned sewing machine, Mrs. Stanford monitored our progress and walked around to provide her assistance. In fact, she had a system where we could write our names on the chalkboard whenever we needed her help. Mine should have been written with a permanent marker. I was domestically challenged. Although I maneuvered my way through trigonometry without too much trouble, Mrs. Stanford's class was a different story.

For some reason, the cooking and sewing stuff did not come naturally to me. I remember having difficulties from the very beginning. One of our first assignments was to make a denim doll. To create this masterpiece, we were supposed to cut the doll pattern out of an old pair of blue jeans and then sew on some orange yarn to serve as hair. That sounded simple enough, but to someone like me, this turned out to be quite a challenge.

I'm not sure how I managed to mess this up, but when I turned my denim doll inside out, she was bald. I'd somehow sown the strands of orange yarn inside my doll. To this day, I have no idea how I managed that one.

Obviously, I had issues when it came to sewing. In addition to having trouble figuring out the sewing patterns, I could not sew six inches without creating a pucker. I can still hear Mrs. Stanford's voice as she would inspect my work and then reply, "Looks like you have some puckers. Take these out with your seam ripper." Throughout the semester, I began to think of the seam ripper as just another appendage.

When I think back to the sewing projects, the thing that stands out the most was the Sulligent High School Fashion Show. This was an event Mrs. Stanford orchestrated each year in which we would model the outfits we'd made in Home

Economics. And much to our dismay, this modeling took place on stage, in front of the entire school body.

I remember working on a knit vest and matching pair of navy pants to wear during the infamous show. It had taken me the majority of the semester to create this suit, since I had used the seam ripper more times than I can remember. So, after sewing, taking apart, and sewing again, I finally finished the vest and pair of pants just in time for the SHS Fashion Show. And things were going along just fine until I remembered I had to iron the outfit one last time. Although Mrs. Stanford had always instructed us to use a press cloth when we were ironing, I chose to ignore her advice. I thought it just seemed like a big waste of time.

I should have known better.

I'm not exactly sure how I managed this. I suppose I allowed the iron to get too hot or just left it in one spot too long. All I know is that when I finished with my ironing, I noticed I'd left an imprint of the iron, with steam holes and all, on the front of my vest.

I motioned for Grace to come over to see if she noticed anything unusual. When Grace was about ten feet away she asked, "What's that big shiny spot?"

I replied, "Hush. Mrs. Stanford will hear you."

Then Grace asked, "So how are you going to fix *that*?"

About that moment, Mrs. Stanford approached and simply asked, "What happened to your vest?"

I whispered, "Well, I didn't use a press cloth…this time."

Mrs. Stanford politely informed me I'd have to wear my outfit, shiny or not. And so I did. In April of 1980, I wore my homemade outfit, with a prominent shiny imprint, in front of the entire SHS student body and made my own fashion statement.

I remember other mishaps like the time Grace and I turned on the garbage disposal and heard this horrible clinging sound. Having never been exposed to the concept of a garbage disposal until that very moment, we reached down in the disposal to inspect what had happened. Somehow, we'd managed to drop a spoon into the disposal; all that was left after it swirled around the disposal for a minute or so was a mangled piece of metal.

And I remember the time Anna burned one of the painted eyes off of the doll she'd made in Mrs. Stanford's class when she was busy talking to Kathryn and inadvertently positioned the blow dryer too close to the doll's face. I also recall the time Grace and I somehow destroyed the heavy-duty bread mixer when we neglected to give our undivided attention to our assigned task and allowed the dough to creep up the beaters and then up in the mixer itself. I also remember the day Grace branded one of Mrs. Stanford's wooden spoons when she decided to use this utensil to lift up a hot oven's heating element. And my friends will never let me forget the day the blueberry muffins exploded in the oven due to the fact that I added fresh blueberries to the muffin dough *after* this mixture had been poured into the individual tins, instead of folding in these ingredients as Mrs. Stanford had instructed.

From the above accounts, one might assume that we were left unsupervised most of the time. That was not the case. Mrs. Stanford constantly checked with each group to make sure things were going as she'd planned. The problem was us; we managed to have issues the moment she walked over to assist another group. We can't blame Mrs. Stanford for any of this. In fact, Mrs. Stanford was one of the most effective teachers I've ever had. She might be surprised to learn that my friends and I actually took in more than these stories seem to convey. Due to her influence, I can differentiate between Chippendale and Hepplewhite, between Queen Anne and Eastlake, and between Sheraton and Duncan Phyfe furniture. I also learned how to properly set a table for a formal dinner party, how to design a simple blueprint for a home, and how to select decorative accessories for a room.

I also learned some effective teaching strategies from her. I learned to have high expectations for my students. I learned to accept that people have varying ability levels. And I learned that I should be accessible to my students. After all, every now and then, they need a little guidance and perhaps a bit of crisis management.

Phone Pranks

In the town of Detroit, Alabama with its population of less than three hundred, people are aware of their neighbors' business. Some residents know more than others. In fact, a few were notorious for their finely tuned abilities to acquire detailed information about each and every individual within a thirty-mile radius. We have often joked that perhaps these individuals should work for the CIA, since their abilities to obtain information seemed so well-refined.

One neighbor in particular stands out in my mind. This neighbor voluntarily kept our parents apprised of our whereabouts, so my brother and his best friend Jake decided that she should be the victim of their next prank. One afternoon, when the guys were young teenagers, they devised a plan and phoned this particular neighbor. Willy made the first call, disguising his voice as an employee of the local phone company.

"This is the phone company. We have a man working on the lines this afternoon, so if your phone rings in the next hour, please do not answer it because it will electrically shock the man on the line."

Confused by this request, yet eager to perform her civic duty, our neighbor agreed to sacrifice her phone conversations for the next sixty or so minutes.

A few minutes later, Willy and Jake took one look at each other and called the neighbor back. They let the phone ring for at least ten minutes. Knowing how irritating a ringing phone could be and how she must be chomping at the bit to answer it, they continued this scenario several times throughout the hour. Since she did not want to shock anyone, our neighbor used some self-control and refused to answer the phone. However, if she had decided to pick up the phone, Jake had devised a plan to yell into the receiver.

"Hang up! Hang up! You're shocking the workman on the line!"

Perhaps our neighbor knew who it was; I guess we will never know because up until this story was written, it was one of the few best-kept secrets in town.

Pretending to work for the local phone company was one of the favorite pranks my brother Willy and his friend Jake played. One afternoon, the guys concocted a new twist. Jake called a neighbor and carefully disguised his voice.

"Today we will be blowing out the lines. To keep debris from collecting all over your house, please put your phone receiver into a pillowcase."

The elderly man, who was quite puzzled by this request, simply asked, "What about putting it in a paper poke? I don't want to mess up any of my pillowcases."

Jake replied, "Yes, a paper poke will work just fine. Just be sure to secure it tightly around the phone receiver so the debris won't come into your house and make a mess."

Without questioning this strange request, the man simply responded, "Okay then, let me go see if I can find me one of them pokes."

The guys promptly called the elderly man back fifteen minutes later and got a busy signal.

Other phone pranks included calling Randy, our Sunday school teacher.

"Is your wife Emily in the apple tree? I believe I spotted her up there on a limb as I passed by your house.

We always managed to find a way to entertain ourselves…so there was never a dull moment in Detroit, Alabama.

Nita Lake

This collection of stories would be remiss if I failed to share about our trips to Nita Lake in Fulton, Mississippi. Like most fathers, our dad enjoyed spending time with us; therefore, when summer approached, Daddy would take a group of us in the family LTD over to Nita Lake for the entire day. The lake promptly opened at ten o'clock each morning and closed at six o'clock each evening. Waiting at the gate, we were there the moment the lake opened and were among the very last to leave.

Daddy enjoyed being out in the sun and often said, "It's good to get a little sun." Perhaps, in some ways, he was right. Studies have shown that the sun does provide Vitamin D. Well, if this is true, we certainly got our share of this particular vitamin. Since we were not well-informed about the damaging effects of the sun's rays in the 1970s, we had no reservations about spending the entire day basking in the sun, soaking up our ample supply of Vitamin D.

Nita Lake was equipped with real beach sand, a few plastic reclining chairs, a handful of beach umbrellas, and two diving boards, one we referred to as the high dive. At the rear of the lake, painted metal containers that resembled oil barrels were connected together with some sort of cable wire and were labeled with the lake's depth. The distance from the sand to the barrels was approximately twenty-five yards or so.

One of our favorite things to do was to get on our inexpensive plastic floats and paddle out to the barrels. Once we were there, we would just hang on to the metal cords that held the barrels together and ride the waves created by the nearby skiers. The only problem we had was getting on the floats, since we usually smothered ourselves in baby oil once we arrived. After sliding off our floats a few times, we would finally figure out a way to stay on and then float out to the barrels. The barrels, if I remember correctly, were labeled with depths of around eighteen feet or so. Since we could swim to some degree and had our trusty floats, we were rarely afraid of the lake's depth. Well, to be honest, I was often afraid; however, Jessica and her cousin Marie seldom were.

Jessica and Marie were always much more adventurous than me. They both wanted to jump off the high dive. I, on the other hand, had absolutely no desire to do so. Therefore, in an effort to add some adventure to my life, Jessica devised a plan. She simply looked at me and asked, "Why don't you just walk over to the high dive and stand next to me so I won't be by myself?"

Like a dummy, I agreed and stood next to her in line.

"Now that you're over here, walk up the ladder with me," she said.

Without thinking, I did so. Once we reached the top, I had planned to just walk back down the ladder, but, of course, my plan didn't work out. After reaching the top of the ladder, Jessica looked back at me.

"Since you are up here, you might as well jump. You can't go back down now. Look down at all those people on the ladder. You can't walk past them."

I should have known better.

Realizing that jumping was probably my only alternative, I followed Jessica and began to tentatively walk down the diving board. I honestly don't remember how high this diving board was. At the time, it seemed like at least fifty feet above the water. All I remember is that I closed my eyes, said a prayer, and plunged like a cannonball into the lake's waters. Jessica and Marie, on the contrary, did cannonballs off the high dive, on purpose. I just watched from a distance, along with Grace.

Once, when I was away at college, my friend Grace, for some unknown reason, decided she would take my brother Willy and his friend Jake to Nita Lake. Little did she know what an experience that would be. Wanting to make good time and arrive by ten o'clock, Grace didn't exactly drive the speed limit in her mom's pea green Malibu. As she topped a hill and rounded a curve, she noticed workmen in the road waving bright orange flags, signaling for her to stop. Willy and Jake did not miss a beat. They hung out the car windows, waved back and forth with their arms, and yelled.

"No brakes! No brakes!"

The horrified construction workers dove into the ditch as the Malibu kept going without the slightest loss in acceleration. They arrived at the lake at ten o'clock, just as planned.

After they had paid their admission and collected all their belongings, Grace was in for more. Jake decided he would attach his beach towel around his shoulders and run up and down the beach, pretending he was Captain Marvel. Grace, who was nineteen at the time, tried to ignore Jake as he yelled, "Shazam!" to the lake's visitors. Embarrassed by this whole Captain Marvel routine, Grace pretended that she didn't know who he was. Jake, of course, wouldn't allow it. Throughout the rest of the day, Jake went to great lengths to make sure everyone was aware he knew Grace, and he had ridden over to the lake with her that particular day.

I believe sometime that afternoon Jake was paid back. Somehow when people purchased things at the concession stand, they automatically entered your name in a drawing for a prize. About three o'clock that afternoon, the concession stand made an announcement on the loudspeaker that could be heard all over the lake.

"Jake Cash is the fine recipient of a box of moon pies. Come to the concession stand, Jake, and claim your fine moon pies."

Jake pretended not to hear.

They made a second announcement.

"Jake Cash, the moon pies are here waiting for you; they're delicious."

To put an end to the embarrassment, Jake walked up to the concession stand to claim his prize. Grace says she can still remember Jake walking back down the beach, hunched over with his eyes staring at the sand, carrying a new box of moon pies. She remembered thinking it was poetic justice.

I also remember how Grace and I would position her sister Kathryn as "bait" to lure guys in our direction. Kathryn was five years younger than the rest of us and could hold her own in any Southern beauty contest. All Kathryn had to do was to just walk around innocently. In the blink of an eye, every eligible bachelor on the beach would congregate around her like Scarlett O'Hara in the opening scene of *Gone with the Wind*. Grace and I, who were always positioned nearby, would then strike up a conversation with the guys who just couldn't seem to work their way into Kathryn's line of sight.

Other memories spring to mind that include talking with a guy named Dawson, who actually had a ski boat and visited the lake each year, just like my friends and I did. Dawson had a friend named Mitch that really had an eye for Jessica, but since we were only about fourteen at the time, it never developed into anything but harmless flirting, Southern-style.

I also remember leaving the lake charred, like a red lobster. Since my brother and I are of Irish/English decent, we have very fair complexions. And when you add to this equation the fact that we only used baby oil mixed with iodine, one can do the math. Since SPF of 40 was not available at this time, Willy and I soon learned to compensate by spending more time at the concession stand, which had picnic tables and a large tin roof to shelter us from the sun's blistering effects.

When I visualize this concession stand, I see Daddy pouring out all of his change on the picnic table and telling each of us, "Take as much money as you need and get whatever food you want." And, I can still picture Jake and Jessica's shocked faces as they stared at the coins and tried to comprehend that Daddy wanted them to take all they wanted as well. Daddy was generous with what little he had and loved Jake and Jessica as his own. Although Daddy only made minimum wage at his job, he always loved being able to do what he could for his children and their friends. Daddy was one of a kind. As I picture this scene in my mind, I feel a tug at my heart as I think about all the sacrifices he made for us...

Not only did Daddy take us to the lake, but Ken did as well. I remember riding along in the avocado green Impala one day with Jessica, Jake, and Willy. In this huge 70s automobile, there was plenty of room for us all to spread out. On this particular occasion, Jake and Willy sat in the front seat beside Ken, leaving plenty of room in the backseat for Jessica and myself. While we were making our way to Nita Lake, I remember Jessica and Jake giving their father a hard time about the Impala. It was a few years old and cramped their style. Ken, being the wise and frugal man that he was, assured them the automobile was perfectly fine and rode like a dream. Moments after these words left his mouth we had reason to think otherwise.

As we traveled down the road to Nita Lake, we forgot to tell Ken that the last turn was soon approaching. When we were about ten feet from the turn, we realized this and yelled, "Turn left!" To make the turn, I remember Ken slamming on the brakes, as the Impala seemed to make a left turn while in mid-air. As soon as he slammed on the brakes, the car seat somehow flew forward and pushed Ken's 6'4" frame up into the steering wheel.

In my mind, I can still picture Ken, Willy, and Jake's expressions as they were instantly sandwiched between the dashboard and the seat. Willy and Jake sat only inches from the windshield, in shock, with their mouths agape and eyes as big as half-dollars. There was silence.

After coming to a stop, Ken readjusted the seat as we all tried to readjust our composure. Jessica and I really wanted to laugh. Ken looked funny with his knees all jammed under the dashboard, but we knew better than to laugh at that moment.

While I really cannot remember what else transpired at the lake that day, I do remember the ride home. As we made our journey back to Detroit, the relentless comments about the need for a new car started again as Jessica and Jake tried to make their case. Ken continued to remain steadfast in his stance for keeping the Impala. I can still hear stating that the vehicle was *dependable*.

A few miles later, we passed a truckload of teenagers; being teenagers ourselves, we did the "mature" thing and made faces at them. Moments later, we hit a pothole the diameter of a basketball and blew out a tire. As luck would have it, while we stood stranded on the side of the road as Ken replaced the blown tire with a spare, the same truckload of teenagers drove by and returned the favor by making faces and laughing hysterically at us.

By the way, a few weeks later, the Cash family pulled up into our church's parking lot…in a brand new Cutlass Supreme.

Confetti in the Pines

As autumn approached each year, there were always a few constants: the changing of the landscape from green to a kaleidoscope of orange, crimson, purple, and gold; the smell of burning leaves; the display of mums and pumpkins on front doorsteps; the sounds of the high school band practicing on the football field, and toilet paper dangling from tree limbs, blowing in the breeze.

Since toilet paper was relatively inexpensive, rolling yards was an affordable form of entertainment. One autumn, Jessica and I decided to entertain ourselves by rolling Mrs. Stanford's yard. At the time, I was a sophomore enrolled in a Home Economics class under the direction of Mrs. Stanford at Sulligent High. Given that Mrs. Stanford lived in our small town of Detroit and was somehow related to Jessica, we decided we'd roll her yard. For some strange reason, we only rolled the yards of people we really liked.

After we'd reached this decision, we collected toilet paper for a couple of months and carefully stashed away the rolls in the basement of Jessica's house. Jessica also had another bright idea.

"Let's cut up a bunch of confetti," said Jessica.

I should have known better.

Nonetheless, I listened and spent several afternoons in Jessica's basement cutting up one of her mom's thick catalogs into miniature pieces and then storing the confetti in a white plastic garbage bag. When the bag was completely full, we decided we were ready. Since we were only fifteen years old at the time, neither of us could *legally* drive. Somehow we remedied this situation by talking some guy friends of ours in to taking us over to Mrs. Stanford's house one Saturday night.

That night, we decided to park the car about twenty yards from Mrs. Stanford's house, alongside Highway 17. Slowly we crept into her yard, like military personnel planning a surprise attack, armed with rolls of toilet paper and a bag filled with catalog confetti. With our toilet paper in hand, we started to work, throwing the rolls of paper ten feet or so into the air, directly aiming at individual limbs of the pine trees that surrounded us. As the rolls would fall onto the ground, we'd pick them up again, and repeat the whole process until each strand of paper was hanging from a tree limb. Someone in the group took the white garbage bag of confetti, punched a hole in the bottom of the bag, and ran around scattering tiny shreds of paper all over the yard, laden with pine straw. When we were finished, we stood back to carefully admire our creation.

Long white strands of toilet paper hung from almost every tree limb; the ground was completely covered in the white confetti. To us, it resembled a blanket of freshly fallen snow. Mrs. Stanford, as we would later find out, did not see it this way.

After finishing the yard, Jessica and I reminded the guys it was time for us to return to my house. As we drove up into my front yard, Jessica and I wanted to hastily say goodnight and go inside, but the guys we were with had somehow misinterpreted our intentions and thought that we were actually interested in them. They leaned over to give us a kiss goodnight. We hadn't planned on this. Luckily for us, at precisely that very moment, Jessica's older brother Clint and his friend Tom sped past my house in Clint's black truck, honking and yelling out of the truck windows. This was just what we needed to throw the guys off guard.

At a record pace, we both bounded from the car faster than speeding bullets. Jessica even tore a small hole in her jeans in her haste to exit the car. Once we were inside my house, we thought the worst was over. *We, of course, were wrong.*

At school on Monday, somehow word had gotten out about our little escapade. Secrets rarely stay buried in Detroit, Alabama. Mrs. Stanford was not a happy camper. She instructed me to stay after class and began to lecture me on how disappointed she was in my actions. The disappointment talk was always the ultimate torture. I was mortified and therefore promised to clean up the mess we had created. After school, I promptly found Jessica and told her about what had happened. She agreed to help me clean up the mess, but we realized there was another problem.

We could not legally drive over to Mrs. Stanford's house.

Somehow I conjured up some story and told my dad that I had actually volunteered to help clean up my teacher's yard. He never questioned this, but I suspect deep down he really knew the truth. Without hesitation, he drove me over to Mrs. Stanford's house and told me he'd be back in a couple of hours to pick me up.

After I climbed out of the family LTD, I remember slowly meandering over to the front door and ringing the doorbell. I could feel my face turning red from the embarrassment. Mrs. Stanford, dressed casually in her blue jeans, answered the door and actually gave me a little smile. Once I saw her smile, I felt a little relieved and again apologized, profusely. She simply told me that she had forgiven me, but that she expected me to clean up the enormous mess I'd made. She then handed me a rake and several black garbage bags. I went to work.

Since the trees in her yard were pine trees and this was late autumn, the clean up was even more difficult. Pine straw was everywhere. As I raked, the only way to gather all the confetti was to collect the pine straw as well. The pine straw was knee deep, almost. I remember raking the pine straw into a small mound and bending down to stuff it into thirty-gallon garbage bags.

Thoughts ran through my mind: What were we thinking when we cut up these microscopic pieces of paper? Where is Jessica anyhow?

About that time, Laura drove up in the Cutlass with Jessica perched in the front seat. As Laura walked over toward me, she had this little smirk on her face, which seemed to say, "Guess you two got caught." Laura walked up to the front porch, rang the doorbell, and struck up a conversation with Mrs. Stanford. We listened to them laugh and were relieved that at least someone was having a good time. Laura returned to her car a few minutes later and instructed Jessica to call her when we were finished.

After waving good-bye to Laura and obtaining another rake from Mrs. Stanford, Jessica began to help me with this monumental task. The more we raked, the larger the yard became in our minds. The one-acre lot seemed more like ten. We thought we'd never finish raking. In no time, we were sweating and had pine straw sticking all over our clothes and in our hair, much like old scarecrows stuck out in a hay field.

To make matters worse, Mrs. Stanford's yard was adjacent to Highway 17, the main route through our town. Thus, as people from our area passed her house, they recognized us and waved, honked, and yelled in our direction. We were beyond embarrassed. I'm sure they knew we weren't out there for community service purposes.

After a couple of hours had passed, Mrs. Stanford came outside and told us to put away the rakes and to come inside the house.

"You may save the rest for the guys to clean up."

Relieved, we walked up on the porch, handed her our rakes, and apologized again. Mrs. Stanford responded, "Let's go inside for some hot cocoa." I remember thinking it was the best hot cocoa I'd ever tasted.

After a few minutes had passed, Jessica tentatively asked if she could call her mom. Once we'd made arrangements for our parents to pick us up, we continued to make small talk and waited for what seemed like an eternity for Laura and James to arrive.

When we heard the sound of our family cars in the driveway, we bolted for the front door like firemen responding to a call and made our way over to the LTD and the Cutlass in the hopes that Mrs. Stanford wouldn't say any more to our parents. Once we were situated in our respective cars, we waved good-bye as our parents slowly backed out of Mrs. Stanford's driveway. I remember Daddy looking over at me and asking, "So how'd it go?"

With pine straw stuck all over me, I replied, "Boy, that's one tough yard to clean."

Daddy just smiled as we made our way back home.

◆   ◆   ◆

Ironically, six years later, I was hired by Mrs. Stanford's husband for my first teaching assignment at Detroit Elementary and even ended up teaching their son, Justin, a few years later.

A Good Samaritan

Rolling yards was a common pastime in our neck of the woods since we had all the necessary ingredients: toilet paper and lots of trees. In fact, it was so common that it was an art form, perfected by my brother and his friends.

On more than one occasion, Willy, Jake, and Phillip decided to roll the yard of one of their classmates at Sulligent High. Actually, for eight weeks straight, the guys rolled this particular yard each and every weekend. This particular night, the guys really took the time to do it right. They used cases of toilet paper. By the time the job was finished, each tree limb of the two-acre lot was meticulously wrapped in white paper and resembled an Egyptian mummy.

When their supply of toilet paper was finally exhausted, the guys made a dash for Willy's Mustang. As they situated themselves in their seats and prepared for a quick get away, Willy turned the ignition key. Nothing happened. With his mouth hanging open, Jake stared over in Willy's direction. Willy turned the ignition key again.

Nothing.

Their adrenalin started to rise. There they were, stalled near Mary's freshly rolled yard, with the evidence of their mischief blowing lightly in the breeze. So, their minds started to race as they tried to generate a solution to this problem.

"Let's try to push it off," suggested Jake.

Jake and Phillip bailed from the car and started to push the car a foot or so at a time as Willy steered the Mustang, moving less than a mile an hour, down Highway 17. About this time, out of nowhere, a kind man stopped to offer his assistance.

The stranger opened up the hood and soon managed to get the car started. As he was about to leave, the Good Samaritan glanced over to the two-acre lot behind the Mustang and could not help but notice the cases of toilet paper billowing in the breeze.

"Good night alive! Somebody got that yard real good!"

As toilet paper formed a backdrop behind them like a white curtain, the guys simply replied, "Yes, sir. Guess that's pretty common…this time of year."

Love at First Sight

I believe in love at first sight; it happened to one of my best friends...

For most of her life, Mrs. Maggie, Jessica's grandmother, lived in a pictur-esque Victorian home along Highway 17, adjacent to our former elementary school. We spent many Sunday afternoons after church in her kitchen, enjoying her homemade meals that always consisted of homegrown vegetables with the best fried chicken, pound cake, fried apple pies, and rolls in the state of Alabama. Mrs. Maggie was undoubtedly one of the best cooks around and was known not only for her cooking but for her candidness as well.

After we'd finished one of Mrs. Maggie's infamous meals, Jessica and I decided we needed some exercise, so we went for a walk and ventured just a few feet away from the Victorian house over to Detroit Elementary School. As we approached the school building, a blue car slowly pulled up beside us. Jessica turned her head to one side to get a glimpse of the driver. She recognized the driver instantly; it was Jack Steele, a guy in her class whom she secretly adored. The car came to a stop. And that's where this story really begins...

Turned out, Jack and his friend Andrew were out cruising around our small town on this particular Sunday afternoon. After shifting the gear to park, Jack rolled down the window and asked, "So what are you two doing out here?"

Jessica tried to contain her enthusiasm as she said, "We're just out and about, getting some exercise."

The conversation between Jack and Jessica progressed while I sort of stared at the ground and kicked around a few pebbles.

A few minutes later, I remember Jack asking Jessica, "Would you both like to ride around Detroit with us?"

Jessica glanced over in my direction like she'd just won the lottery and then gave me *the look*. At that moment, I knew I really did not have a choice.

To let Jessica's parents know what we were up to, the four of us walked back over to Mrs. Maggie's, only to see the entire family including Mrs. Maggie, Mr. Wes, Samantha, Shirley Ree, Dolly, Laura, and Ken all sitting on the front porch drinking some sweet tea and staring over in our direction. As we stepped up onto the porch, we tentatively introduced our new acquaintances and then proceeded to play twenty questions about their parents and all the other members of their family tree. The guys passed round one of the interrogation series, so we received a nod of approval from both Ken and Laura.

After promising to be back in an hour or so, Jack opened the car door and Jessica didn't hesitate to position herself in the front seat next to Jack, leaving me to climb into the backseat next to his friend Andrew. As I made my way to the backseat of the car, I made a mental note that his friend was seated on one side of the car, right behind Jessica. Since I had no intentions of sitting next to a perfect stranger, I purposely positioned myself on the opposite side of the backseat, right behind Jack.

While Jessica and Jack's conversation seemed to be going well, the one I was having with Andrew was not. To make matters worse, Andrew started inching his way over to my side of the car, little by little, like a snake, encroaching on my space. I moved in the opposite direction, closer and closer to the door, hoping that he would get the hint. He missed this hint or simply chose to ignore it. And so, he continued to slowly slither across the car seat in my direction. I felt like an insect that had just gotten caught in a web. I was trapped. I remember looking out the car window, wondering how critically I'd be hurt if I opened the car door and jumped. As I contemplated my fate, I made ugly faces at Jessica in the rearview mirror.

Jessica, of course, pretended not to notice.

After about an hour or so, which seemed like an eternity to me, the guys took us back to Mrs. Maggie's house and promised to call us later. While Jack asked for Jessica's phone number, I gladly volunteered some information to Andrew: I didn't have a telephone…

◆　　　◆　　　◆

As for Jessica and Jack, it was love at first sight. They were married six years later and continue to live happily ever after.

Double Dates

When we were around the age of sixteen, Jessica's parents appropriately encouraged us to go on double dates. Since I was not dating anyone at the time, I was fortunate (sometimes unfortunate) enough to go out with most of Jack's friends. While I have somehow forgotten many of these dates, some do stand out in my mind more than others...

One Saturday night I decided that I would pamper myself with a hot bubble bath, a facial mask, and a pedicure. I remember pinning up my hair with bobby pins, smearing a thick green mud mask on my face, and stepping into my hot bubble bath. I had been in the tub for no more than five minutes when someone started pounding on the bathroom door.

It was Jessica.

As I hurriedly grabbed my robe and opened the door, Jessica looked at me, laughed, and then whispered, "Tina, get ready."

"What in the world for?" I asked.

"Because you have a date waiting out in the living room, that's why."

"A what?" I asked as I stared at Jessica in disbelief with my green mud mask smeared across my face.

She explained that her mom really wanted me to go on a double date with them so Jack had brought one of his friends along for me. Since we did not have a telephone, there was no way to convey this information to me ahead of time.

"Who is he?" I asked.

Jessica just frantically motioned me to my room. "I'll explain everything as you're getting ready. Hurry up now, they're out there talking to your dad."

I scanned my closet to find something appropriate to wear while Jessica asked, "What can I do to help you get ready?" I knew this translated into, "Tina, you'd better hurry up!"

As I wiped the green mask from my face and tried to smear on some make-up, I started asking, "What does he look like?" and "How old is he?"

Jessica assured me that he had a great personality and that we'd get along just fine.

After listening to Jessica talk me into going on this date, I somehow threw myself together and tried to look presentable to Jack's friend. I can only imagine what the poor guy was thinking as he overheard our conversation as I tried to blow dry my wet hair.

I honestly don't remember what transpired later that evening, but I do remember that a few weeks after this incident we heard rumors that this particular friend of Jack's was dating a friend of ours from Detroit. Given the probability that my green facial mask was still visible the night of our first date, I can't say that I blame him one bit.

Late Night at the Movies

A few years after the infamous exit from the Gu-Win Drive-In, we had yet another episode, involving different circumstances...

When Jessica and I were around the age of sixteen, we decided to watch a movie at the Gu-Win Drive-In. And, since Jessica was dating Jack at the time, she wanted Jack to go along with us. Like always, I listened and went along with the plan. The only problem with this plan was the fact we'd neglected to tell Jessica's parents that Jack was somehow involved in the equation. We did not lie; we just did not *volunteer* this information.

Once we arrived at the drive-in, we realized that the feature presentation we really wanted to see was to be shown after the first movie. At the time, we did not have access to cellular phones and never really thought about using a pay phone to inform Jessica's parents that we'd be late. Jessica had a curfew of ten-thirty. Somehow this fact did not click in our minds. Without thinking, we decided to wait for the feature presentation, which started at around ten-thirty that night. Since we had paid our admission fees, we thought it would be a shame just to throw away all that money; therefore, we stayed for the duration of each film. The final movie ended a little after midnight.

Meanwhile, the Cash household was in an uproar. Jessica's dad was pacing the floor with his 6'4" frame. He checked the clock at eleven, then at eleven-thirty, and then promptly at twelve midnight. He was not a happy camper. Laura tried to assure him that everything was okay, but Ken understandably envisioned the worst. At one o'clock in the morning, Ken decided to take matters into his own hands, got into the family's brown Cutlass, and headed toward Guin. His route down Highway 17 led him initially to Sulligent where he planned to make a left turn and proceed toward Guin.

After the movie ended at around midnight, Jessica and I drove Jack from Guin, Alabama over to his home in Gattman, Mississippi, drove back to Sulligent, and then stopped at a traffic light before heading across the railroad tracks to Detroit. It was late at night, around one-fifteen or so. We were alone on the streets, except for one approaching vehicle.

Jessica was the first one to recognize the approaching vehicle. It looked familiar.

Uh-oh.

With a knot forming in her throat, Jessica whispered, "It's my Daddy."

Our lives flashed before our eyes.

I then drove my car over to Mr. Cash's brown Cutlass and placed the gear in park. As I glanced in his direction, I couldn't help but notice that one of Ken's pupils was dilated. This was a signature trait that said he was not happy. I tentatively rolled down the window and tried to force a fake smile as Jessica peeked around me. Jessica tried to play innocent.

"What are you doing here, Daddy?"

Ken, resembling Sheriff Andy Taylor from *Mayberry*, gave us both the look.

Without missing a beat, Ken said, "Tina, it's time you went home." Then he stared at Jessica with his dilated eye and said, "Young lady, get in this car right this second."

I remember choking as I replied, "Yes, sir."

As I drove toward Detroit along Highway 17, following closely behind the brown Cutlass, I replayed what had just transpired. Realizing how understandably upset our parents were, I started trying to come up with a way to explain everything to Daddy. Jessica said the ten-mile trip home was one of the longest she can recall. Needless to say, we learned our lesson. From that day forward we never stayed for the late movie. Most importantly, we called when we anticipated we'd be arriving after our curfew.

Just Married

The location and size of our small town was one catalyst in the development of our creativity. Simply put, our afternoons and evenings were rarely spent in malls, theatres, or restaurants; therefore, when we were not in the garden picking peas or corn, we had some extra time on our hands. Occasionally, we used this time to devise some mischievous plans that were, in our eyes, quite clean and wholesome…

One muggy summer night, my friend Grace and I drove by Jessica's house and happened to notice that Jack's yellow and white (AKA "Big Yella") truck was parked in the driveway.

This gave us an idea.

Grace and I figured that after Jack left Jessica's house he would probably do like most teenagers and ride around the block, in the nearby town of Sulligent, before he went home. Knowing that Jack would be alone and therefore riding around the block by himself, we decided to decorate his truck in a special way.

To fully appreciate this story, understand that the town of Sulligent where we attended high school only boasted a population of 2,000 or so. Therefore, when teenagers drove around the only block in town, everyone recognized their vehicle. Anyone who saw the yellow and white truck would associate it with Jack.

Armed with this information, Grace and I decided to decorate Jack's truck as if he'd just been married. We could just picture him riding around town, *alone*, trying to look cool and macho around his peers, oblivious to a "Just Married" sign plastered across the back of his truck.

Knowing that time was of the essence, Grace and I drove a couple of miles over to her house to design our wedding decorations. Somehow we came across some pink and white crepe paper (I think it was left over from the prom) and quickly twisted this stuff in a rope-like fashion to create some streamers. Then we turned our attention to the sign. Taking poster board and some glitter, we spelled out the infamous words and carefully placed the sign along with the streamers in Grace's pea green Malibu. Then we headed toward Jessica's.

As we approached Jessica's house, Grace cleverly decided that we should park her car about fifty yards or so away. With our materials in hand, we carefully made our way over to Jack's truck. Crawling behind the vehicle, we draped the crepe paper streamers along the passenger's side, secured this with some tape, and then made our way over to the tailgate to attach the infamous poster, with huge gold glitter letters, which clearly read, "Just Married."

Throughout the remainder of the weekend, we waited in anticipation to hear how others had reacted to Jack's status as a newlywed. On Monday at school, Jessica shared with us what had actually transpired that night.

As luck would have it, Jack needed to get something out of the back of the truck shortly after we had completed our decorating. When he walked around to the tailgate of the truck, he discovered our decorations. Jessica held her stomach as she laughed and easily put two and two together to determine who was responsible. Being a good sport about the whole thing, Jessica saved the infamous sign and used it on their vehicle a few years later, one day in September of 1985...the day of her wedding.

A Dead Battery and Some Jumper Cables

In the summer of 1980 the latest fashion trend was the preppy look, the television show *Dallas* was a hit series, and we were looking forward to our upcoming senior year.

That particular summer we spent many Sunday afternoons riding around the small town of Hamilton, located about twenty miles from our hometown. Hamilton was the county seat of Marion County, and like other small towns, had its own specific path most teenagers drove around on weekends.

One particular Sunday, Grace and I rode around this infamous path in my Ford Fairmont; it was new and at the time, I was actually proud of this two-door four-cylinder baby blue automobile. As we slowed down to make one of the turns in the loop, a sports car drove up beside us. Some teenage boys leaned out from the window of the automobile and asked us our names. Somehow, they ended up with our phone numbers. A week later, the guys called, and Grace and I agreed to go on a double date with Bryan and Matthew.

The date started off like any other. We drove to Tupelo, Mississippi, an hour drive from our home, to the nearest theatre to watch a movie starring Bill Murray. After the movie, we made the hour drive home, returned to my house, and sat in the car talking and listening to the radio. Being teenagers, we forgot to look at the clock. Little did we know something was about to happen that would remind us what time it actually was...

We saw headlights approaching in the distance; this was odd because my home was located on a remote gravel road that few people traveled. I distinctly remember looking out the car window to identify whose automobile it was. Grace was the first to make out the outline of the truck.

Uh-oh.

It was her mother. And Virginia Mae was racing down our dirt road, creating a cloud of dust, as she headed toward our driveway. As Virginia Mae whipped into the driveway, gravel scattered everywhere. We glanced at the clock; it read thirty minutes past midnight.

This wasn't good.

To make matters worse, in her haste to get out of the pickup truck, Virginia Mae forgot to put the gear in park. As she bounded from the truck, the vehicle started rolling backwards. This, understandably, didn't help her mood. Without missing a beat, she grabbed the door of the truck as it rolled down our driveway, reached in, placed the gear in park, and marched over to us.

We stared at her in disbelief as we witnessed what she'd done with the truck.

I still remember the first words out of Virginia Mae's mouth.

"Grace Anne, do you have any idea what time it is? We've been worried sick about you! Get in the truck, young lady, right this instant!"

Like most of us, Grace was only called by her full name when she was in deep trouble.

Bryan, Matthew, and I stared at Virginia Mae with our mouths wide open. We were speechless. With no time to introduce her date, Grace sauntered over to her mom's truck with her shoulders slumped and eyes focused on the ground. Embarrassed by the whole incident, Grace climbed into the passenger's side and stared straight ahead. As we watched Grace's expression in the windshield, we stood, as if in a trance, as her mom backed out of our driveway and sped down the gravel road, flinging gravel in every direction. Knowing that I should get into my own house before anything else happened, I quickly said goodnight and closed the front door. I thought the worst was over.

I was wrong.

About five minutes later, I heard a knock at the front door. To keep from waking my parents, I remember sprinting to the door. There stood Matthew. He began to tell me that his car battery was dead.

"Dead?" I asked.

He explained that he had mistakenly turned the car ignition key forward so we could listen to the radio, thus killing the battery.

"Do you have any jumper cables?" he asked in sort of a hopeful tone.

I didn't think that we did, but I for some reason I thought Grace's family had some. Since Matthew's car was parked directly behind my blue Fairmont, I got the keys to the family LTD and promptly headed toward Grace's house. I remember pulling up into her driveway at around one o'clock in the morning.

When she came to the door, I explained the problem and asked, "Do you think your dad has any jumper cables we could use?"

She thought her dad did, but after all that had transpired, she understandably didn't want to wake him.

She had an even better idea.

Grace somehow convinced me that it would be okay if we just took the battery off of her father's pickup truck and let Matthew borrow it. At this time of night, this somehow sounded reasonable. I remember helping Grace unhook her dad's battery and lifting the heavy battery out of the truck. Grace grabbed one end as I held onto the other and hauled the truck battery over to the trusty LTD. After the battery was placed in the floorboard of the LTD, we somehow convinced Grace's mom that she needed to ride back with me. At approximately one-thirty in the morning, we made the six-mile journey back to my house.

While I was at Grace's house taking the battery off her father's truck, my daddy woke up and picked up a flashlight to investigate what all the commotion was about. He had opened the front door, stepped out onto the porch, and stared at the two strangers in our front yard. Matthew later told me that my father had walked over to the two guys and had shone the flashlight in their eyes.

"Which one of you is Matthew?"

Bryan promptly pointed a finger at his friend Matthew and choked on his words as he replied, "He is."

As my dad approached, lumps formed in their throats.

My father simply reached out his hand.

"Nice to meet you, Matthew."

As Matthew exhaled a sigh of relief, he extended his hand to my dad and introduced himself.

A few minutes later, Grace and I pulled up into the driveway in the LTD. I noticed the porch light was on and Daddy was standing over near the guys with his flashlight. I could only imagine what had transpired since we had departed.

As we opened the car door, Matthew yelled, "Hope you were able to find some jumper cables!"

"I've got something better," said Grace. "I stole the battery off my dad's truck!"

Looking at each other in disbelief, Matthew and Bryan asked in unison, "You did what?"

Grace and I were only sixteen at the time and were quite ignorant about cars. We had no idea car batteries actually came in different sizes. After taking one look at the battery, Matthew knew it was much too large and carefully placed the battery back in our car. Grace was quick to volunteer another remedy; she knew that her relative, William Earl, who lived about three miles away, would probably have some jumper cables.

At this time of night, we didn't have many options, so in a flash Grace and I, like Tweedledee and Tweedledum, were off again in the LTD on a cable-finding mission. When we pulled up into William Earl's yard, it was about two o'clock. Having been awakened in the middle of the night, William Earl wasn't exactly coherent. We repeated our story several times. Once he realized what we needed, he meandered over to his truck, produced a set of jumper cables, put the jumper cables in our car, and wished us well.

When we returned to my home, it was around two-thirty. As the LTD came to a stop, we emerged from the car, proudly produced the jumper cables, and hoped the guys knew what in the world they should do with them. Within a few minutes, the guys hooked up the jumper cables to the LTD and soon heard the rumbling of the car's engine. After realizing that all was finally well, we waved good-bye as we watched the car pull out of our driveway at around three o'clock.

To this day, I still do not know how to use jumper cables, but I do know that car batteries come in different sizes.

A Close Encounter with a Ditch

As I was driving home the other day, a green Malibu, a 70s model to be exact, sped past me. This triggered a world of memories that have been dormant for quite some time.

In the spring of 1981, our senior year at Sulligent High, Grace and I were practicing our cheerleading routines in the gym when we glanced over and saw Jessica slowly approaching through the double doors near the front of the gymnasium. We noticed she'd been crying and wanted to talk with us. When we saw the tears, Grace and I immediately assumed she'd had an argument with Jack.

This was not the case.

When Jessica meandered over to us, she glanced around the room, carefully avoiding eye contact with Grace, as the details of the following story began to unravel.

As Jessica was driving Grace's Malibu around town, somehow Jack had ended up in the car with her. The two of them had decided to drive around a residential neighborhood in Sulligent, only a couple of miles from our campus, and at some point along their drive, Jessica sped around a curve a little too fast. In later years, Jessica has confessed to saying, "Let's see what this baby can do!"

In the blink of an eye, the Malibu was in a ditch, stuck on its side. Jessica tried to open the door, but the driver's side was wedged in the ditch, so Jack tried to open the passenger's door. The car was stuck on its side at about a 45-degree angle, so that exit was next to impossible. After several minutes, they managed to crawl through the window on the driver's side.

As luck would have it, Coach Rogers, Jessica's Driver's Education teacher at the time, was driving by in a school bus and caught a glimpse of them climbing out the car's window. Coach Rogers stopped the bus to retrieve Jack, his star basketball player. Sulligent had a game that night.

When Coach Rogers emerged from the bus, he yelled in Jessica's direction.

"How in the world can someone make an A+ in Driver's Education and then run into a ditch?"

Coach Rogers then approached the wreckage and somehow managed to drive the wrecked car out of the ditch.

Although they were not hurt physically, Jessica was a little shaken up; therefore, Jack got behind the wheel of the wrecked Malibu and drove Jessica over to our school campus, but since it was the night of the game and the buses were waiting on Jack, he had to quickly climb aboard one of the buses and leave Jessica at the gym.

Jessica then entered the gym to tell Grace the bad news.

After listening to the story and asking if she was okay, we followed Jessica outside to inspect the damaged Malibu. As we left the gym, Grace was thinking that perhaps the damage wasn't that noticeable.

She was wrong.

The driver's side of the Malibu was all dented in; even the roof had dents. It looked like a slab of beef that had been pulverized with a meat tenderizer. The outside metal mirror was merely dangling by a cord. Grace just stared in disbelief as Jessica profusely apologized once more.

Knowing how her mother would understandably react, Jessica had the idea that we should drive the Malibu over to First State Bank so her mom could initially see the car, in front of her colleagues. Jessica, being the smart person she is, knew that her mom would respond to this crisis calmly as long as her colleagues were around. So we climbed into the dented up, mirror-dangling Malibu and pulled into the bank's drive-through.

I can still picture Laura's expression in the drive-through window. When she spotted our car, her eyes grew as large as half-dollars as her lips mouthed the words, "What in the world?" Seconds later, Jessica's mother met us at the back-door of the bank and asked, "Grace, what happened to your car, sweetie?"

It was at this point that Jessica leaned across me and whispered, "Mama, I had an accident just now. I'm afraid I somehow wrecked Grace's car."

Laura quickly responded with a host of questions: "What in the world?" "Are you all right?" "What happened?" "Why were you driving Grace's car?"

After Jessica replayed the events that had transpired once more, Laura was relieved that no one was hurt and acted as though it wasn't a big deal. *But we knew better.*

Sandwiched between Jessica and Grace, the ten-mile trip home was memorable. As we approached the first traffic light and pulled to a stop, the mirror that was dangling by a cord banged up against the car door and made a sound much like a cowbell. I couldn't help it. I laughed like I'd never laughed before. Tears ran down my face. Every time we stopped, the dangling mirror would knock up against the door and ding. From my vantage point, I could see the mirror out of the driver's side window as it dangled back and forth. When we crossed the railroad tracks, it made a few clanging sounds, almost in rhythm. I laughed some more.

Grace just gave me the look as Jessica whispered, "Tina, it's not funny." It was certainly funny to me. Problem was, I found myself in a situation where I wasn't supposed to laugh; this only made matters worse. Every time I caught a glimpse of the dangling mirror, I would hold my breath, in an attempt to suppress my giggling, only to blow out all the air, like deflating a balloon. Grace and Jessica, of course, were not amused.

As we made the ten-mile journey home, Grace and Jessica talked about how they would break the news to Grace's mother. They also knew they'd have to tell their fathers, but as luck would have it, their fathers were out of town *together* on a business trip and would not be back for a couple of days. Telling them would have to wait.

Somehow they talked me into being with them when they shared the news with Grace's mom. Virginia Mae had taught the three of us in first grade and still had a command of presence about her that made us all feel as though we should stand at attention. When we drove up into the yard, Grace's mother was out in the front yard burning leaves. Virginia Mae glanced up from the fire, smiled, and waved in our direction. Seconds later, she glanced in our direction again. This time, she cocked her head sideways as her expression changed.

Virginia Mae approached with a purpose, holding onto her rake like a vice grip. As she made her way over in our direction, the car came into full focus.

"Grace Anne, what in the world have you done young lady?"

Jessica looked over in her direction, stammered around, and nervously said, "Virginia Mae, Grace didn't do this. I did."

I remember Virginia Mae listening to Jessica's explanation as she walked around the car, at a snail's pace, touching each indention and inspecting every inch. She inspected the dangling mirror. This time, I didn't laugh.

Once the inspection was done, we all returned home, only to wait for the return of Ken and William from their business trip. Their mothers had decided not to share this information with them over the phone but rather allow them to hear it firsthand from their daughters. Jessica later shared with me what transpired when she initially told Ken.

After Ken had unpacked his things and had eaten one of Laura's delicious home-cooked meals, Jessica got up her nerve.

"Daddy, I need to talk to you about something. While you were gone on your trip, I sort of wrecked…"

Before she could finish her sentence, Ken dashed toward the garage to inspect the family car.

Jessica whispered, "No, Daddy. It wasn't our car. It was Grace's."

"Grace's car? What in the world were you doing driving Grace's car?"

It was at this point that Ken ordered Jessica to get in the car with him and to drive over to the Alexander residence to make things right. This two-mile drive seemed to last forever, although they arrived at Grace's house in a matter of minutes. Jessica endured more humiliation as the car was meticulously inspected by her father and the story was retold once more.

The Malibu story, though, does have a happy ending. The Malibu was quickly repaired, no one was physically hurt, and to my knowledge this was Jessica's last encounter with a ditch.

A Trip to the Big Easy

This was one trip that was anything but easy...

During the summer of 1981, our pastor, Kevin Johnson, decided to attend seminary in the city of New Orleans. And for some unknown reason, Kevin decided to take three teenage guys along with him on a brief road trip to visit the seminary's campus.

This, of course, was a mistake.

In fact, I have no idea why he chose to take Willy, Jake, and Phillip along with him to experience the sights and culture of New Orleans. Perhaps Kevin thought he would be a positive influence on their lives. Perhaps he thought it would be a cultural experience for them. Perhaps he thought they would be on their best behavior. Perhaps he just wasn't thinking.

The trip began with the guys loading up their luggage into the brown Pinto and positioning themselves just so in the vehicle. Phillip was seated in the front on the passenger's side with Willy and Jake in the backseat.

Early into the six-hour trip, Jake decided to entertain everyone with his jokes, which were corny in nature and thus became old in a matter of minutes. Not to be out done, Willy and Phillip also did their best to entertain the group as Kevin began to realize that perhaps he'd made a big mistake.

After weaving their way from Alabama through the middle of Mississippi and down toward south Louisiana, the guys approached the city known as *The Big Easy*. As they entered the metropolitan area, Kevin asked Phillip to unfold the map and navigate. This was also a mistake.

They drove around for what seemed like hours, perplexed by the fact that the map didn't match the streets. Then Kevin noticed *the source* of the problem.

"Son, you've got the map upside down," said Kevin. "You and Willy swap places."

Seconds later, with Willy in the navigator seat, things were going along just fine until they realized they were going in the wrong direction on the Lake Pontchartrain Causeway.

To remedy this problem, Kevin said, "I'm going to do a U-turn and go in the other direction."

"You'd better not," replied Willy.

"Why not?" asked Kevin

"That's why," said Willy as he pointed to a sign with the words *No U-turn*.

"Do you guys see any cops around?" asked Kevin.

"Nope," replied the guys in unison.

Taking matters into his own hands, Kevin whipped the Pinto around and headed in the other direction on the bridge. Moments later, they heard the following statement announced over a loudspeaker:

"Pull over!"

Since they didn't hear a siren, Kevin kept driving. Thirty seconds later, they heard the following:

"You in the brown Pinto...pull over."

The guys turned their heads around to the see what was behind them and heard, "Yeah, you."

Kevin slowly pulled the Pinto over to the side and carefully rolled down his window to speak with the officer. As Kevin tried to talk his way out of a ticket by mentioning that he was a pastor, Willy decided to open the glove compartment. He plundered around, noticed a sock, and decided to pull the sock out for closer inspection. Kevin caught a glimpse of what Willy was doing.

"What's in this sock?" asked Willy.

"Put that up," Kevin whispered as he gritted his teeth and continued to force a fake smile at the officer.

"It's kind of heavy," commented Willy.

"Put it up," Kevin whispered.

"Wonder why it's so heavy?" asked Willy.

"It's a gun," whispered Kevin, out of the side of his mouth, as he continued to nod and make small talk with the officer.

"Uh-oh," whispered Willy.

As Willy held his breath, he slowly eased the gun back to where he'd found it and carefully closed the glove compartment. Minutes later, the police officer, who seemed satisfied with Kevin's excuse, instructed them to be careful during their stay in New Orleans and walked back toward his car. Once the officer was gone, Kevin gave Willy *the look* as Jake and Phillip laughed and slapped their knees at what had just transpired.

Later that afternoon, they arrived at the campus of the New Orleans Baptist Theological Seminary and decided to tour one of the dorms. As Willy, Jake, and Phillip entered one of the dorms, they noticed the hardwood floors had a few loose boards which made creaking sounds when you tapped them just right. This gave them an idea. As soon as Kevin was out of sight, they stomped up and down the halls in their cowboy boots, hitting every creaking board in sight.

Later that evening, Kevin decided to take the guys sight-seeing. This was also a mistake. As they walked up and down the streets of the French Quarter, they saw much more than they'd planned to see and soon realized that things were different here; they weren't in Kansas anymore.

The next morning, they packed their bags and waved good-bye to New Orleans. As they made their way back home to Alabama, they were making good time until Willy looked down at his right hand.

"I left my class ring back at the restaurant!"

"You did what?" replied Kevin.

"I remember taking it off when I washed my hands."

"That place is 100 miles in the opposite direction!" yelled Kevin.

As a myriad of thoughts ran through his mind, Kevin turned the Pinto around and headed back toward New Orleans to retrieve Willy's class ring. Upon returning to the restaurant, the manager gave Willy back his ring, which someone had found and actually returned.

Thinking that the worst was finally over, the guys situated themselves in the brown Pinto and headed toward home. But, the dark cloud of unfortunate events that seemed to loom over them did not let up.

Along about Mississippi, the brown Pinto experienced some mechanical problems. The guys got out, fiddled around under the hood, and soon realized they were stranded. Kevin decided to call his father.

"Dad, I need for you to come and get us," said Kevin.

"Where 'bouts are you son?" replied his father.

"We're in the middle of Mississippi…about a three-hour drive from home."

"Don't worry; I'll be there as soon as I can."

As promised, Mr. Moore arrived a few hours later and attached the Pinto to his truck with a chain. For the remainder of the trip home, Kevin gripped his hands tightly around the steering wheel of the Pinto and stared straight ahead as the guys sat in the car with him (to keep him company) and jerked back and forth, simultaneously, each time the chain's tension changed.

◆   ◆   ◆

Months later, Kevin enrolled at New Orleans Baptist Theological Seminary and made several trips back and forth to Lamar County. Although the six-hour trip to *The Big Easy* was often lonely, Kevin did not extend any future invitations to Willy, Phillip, or Jake. The memories were enough to keep him company.

A Burning Question

One afternoon, when Grace and I were in our early twenties and living in Florence, we perused the pages of a cookbook and came across a recipe for banana *flambé*. Having dismissed our former mishaps in Mrs. Stanford's Home Economics class, Grace had the bright idea that we should create this flaming dessert.

I should have known better.

After making the decision to *set fire* to a dessert, we opened Grace's kitchen cabinets and located all of the ingredients for our recipe, except one. To ignite our dessert, we needed some rum. Problem was, Grace and I didn't know the first thing about purchasing alcohol, given the fact that we grew up in tee totaling Protestant households in a dry county.

Since we were quite ignorant about alcohol, Grace and I first thought about driving over to the Winn-Dixie (since Grace had noticed some bottles of wine along the grocery store's aisles), but for some reason changed our minds and decided to scan the yellow pages. Grace found one she thought might work and subsequently wrote down the address on a piece of notebook paper. We then positioned ourselves in Grace's Cutlass and made our way over to the chosen store. As we drove up to the parking lot of the liquor store, Grace put on some sunglasses to hide her identity, since she was student teaching at the time.

The moment we walked into the store we marveled at the number of shelves, each filled with glass bottles in a myriad of colors. Since we were overwhelmed with the selections, Grace decided we should ask the guy working behind the counter for some assistance. When we approached, Grace and I noticed he had a gold tooth, which happened to match the thick chain around his neck.

Grace, looking like the epitome of a Southern belle, walked up to the counter and innocently asked, "Do you have any rum?"

He smiled, like the Cheshire Cat, and responded, "Honey, we've got any sort of rum you need. We've got some on this wall and then on that shelf and then there's a whole row of it up against this other wall."

Grace politely said, "Thank you," with her sweet Southern accent and walked with a purpose toward one set of shelves along the back wall.

As we approached the back wall, we found several bottles of rum, just like the guy behind the counter said. We were overwhelmed with the selections. Grace, still hiding behind her sunglasses, carefully examined each bottle of rum, searching for one with the proof number specified in our recipe. The moment she found it, she held the glass bottle up high and exclaimed, "I bet this one will work, but it costs too much!" So, we scanned the shelves for something less expensive. We then came across another bottle of rum priced at only $9.99, with a proof number much less than the previous more expensive bottle.

Since we needed rum that would ignite our dessert, Grace looked at me and asked, "Do you think this cheap one will burn?"

At that moment, a man who'd been watching this whole scenario play out, simply grinned, displaying the few teeth he had, and winked at us as he said, "No ma'am. That stuff will go down real smooth."

And so, we took his advice, made our purchase, and learned a lesson…even the cheap stuff will burn.

PART II
The Same but Different

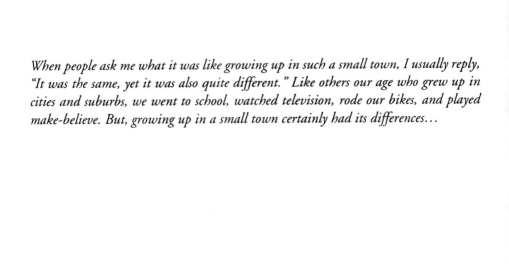

When people ask me what it was like growing up in such a small town, I usually reply, "It was the same, yet it was also quite different." Like others our age who grew up in cities and suburbs, we went to school, watched television, rode our bikes, and played make-believe. But, growing up in a small town certainly had its differences...

Top 20 Ways Life is Different in the Rural South

1. Gun control means locking the glass doors on the gun cabinet.

2. Along the highway, *Cattle Crossing* signs are common; *Exit* signs are rare.

3. There are no privacy fences: Fences are reserved for cattle, pigs, and horses.

4. People drive with their headlights on high beam since streetlights are few and far between.

5. You can burn sticks, limbs, and leaves in your front yard, if you want.

6. There's no such thing as road rage; your main concern is dodging deer along the blacktop.

7. There are no water bills: Outside the city limits, water comes from a well.

8. No business is open 24/7.

9. There are no deed restrictions: You can paint your house any color, put up any type of storage building, and put your garage or carport wherever you want.

10. Honking means, "Hey, y'all."

11. Vegetables are grown in a garden behind the house, not purchased along the aisles of a grocery store.

12. No one owns a fondue pot; every family owns a pressure cooker.

13. Churches have bi-vocational pastors, not full-time ministers.

14. Foods are fried, not steamed.

15. Dinner is served at noon; supper is served in the evening.

16. Trick-or-treating is done by driving from house-to-house, not by dropping off children in the middle of a subdivision.

17. People have a yard, not a lawn.

18. Every household has a clothesline, a pressure cooker, a gun, a freezer, and a King James Version of the Holy Bible.

19. Gardens span acres, not yards.

20. No need for photo identification; everyone knows your name.

Steel Magnolias

Women in our area were certainly similar to ladies in the suburbs in some respects and certainly different in others. They were like Southern magnolias in the sense that they looked feminine, like a delicate flower, especially on Sunday mornings with their high-heeled pumps, their pearl earrings they called "ear bobs," and their tailored dresses. Like ladies in southern suburbs, they hosted bridal and baby showers, smocked baby clothes by hand, and could whip up just about anything from scratch with just a handful of ingredients. On the other hand, they were quite different from the June Cleaver types. They were like steel. These ladies were tough and independent. They were survivors. In fact, had the television series *Survivor* been aired a decade or so back, we would have entered our mothers on this series, in a heartbeat. They, most assuredly, would have walked away with the grand prize…

Mother, who was only 4'11", never weighed more than ninety pounds in her life but was tough to the core. She owned and used the following tools on a regular basis: a sling blade, a chainsaw, a hacksaw, a shovel, a rake, and of course, a garden hoe. Johnson grass never had a fighting chance around Mother. And up until her mid-seventies, Mother mowed her own one-acre yard, with a push mower, until the day we finally took the thing away from her. I can still picture her pushing that mower beyond our yard into an area where only a tractor would survive, mowing down small trees, slinging rocks, and creating a dust storm in her path.

To say that Mother was independent and tough would be quite an understatement. Not only did she refuse to hire anyone to mow the grass, she also refused to hire anyone to paint. Instead, she would climb up on a ladder and paint the walls of her home, all by herself, with a roller attached to a pole taller than she was, all in an attempt to save a few dollars. And, unlike her daughter, Mother wasn't afraid of snakes or anything, for that matter. I've seen her decapitate the head of a copperhead with a garden hoe and then go about her business, cultivating her one-acre garden, like nothing happened. At 4'11", she was one tough woman.

Her tough spirit was a part of her until her final days. Days before she passed away, she had to undergo surgery to repair a hip fracture. Upon waking from the surgery, Mother refused to take an ounce of morphine for pain, claiming that she didn't want to take a chance and get "addicted." I can still picture the surprised look on the physician's face as he stood over her hospital bed and shook his head. "That little lady is one tough cookie."

Another tough cookie is Paula Martin. Now in her early eighties, she's managed to raise five children, teach Sunday school, and watch after several other children in the community through the years, including my brother and myself when we were youngsters. Mrs. Martin, who at her age isn't quite in perfect health, still continues to care for her son who has severe diabetes and has lost his legs to this debilitating disease. Mrs. Martin has outlived her husband and one of her sons, both of whom died from complications related to diabetes, and yet she somehow manages all of this without complaint.

This list of tough women also includes Grace and Kathryn's mom, Virginia Mae, who at the age of 76, purchased a chainsaw so she could "clear some land" around their home place. Well, to be quite honest, this is Virginia Mae's second chainsaw. The first one was secretly taken away by her daughters to protect her, but Virginia Mae didn't blink. She just went out and got herself another one, and it's even bigger than the first.

Virginia Mae spent thirty-three years as a teacher working with elementary-age children, decided to retire, and then decided she'd go back to work. For her second career, she applied for a job at Detroit Slacks garment factory. Here, she worked more than sixty hours a week alongside my mother and Mrs. Maggie, who also refused to quit, even though they were all in their late sixties and early seventies. Virginia Mae was forced to retire from her second job when Detroit Slacks closed its doors a few years back. Had that not been the case, I'd bet she'd still be there, putting in overtime.

Another pioneer-type made of pure steel is Aunt Irene. She is the type of person who recently responded, "Honey, I'm down to only three acres," when I asked about the size of her garden. And up until a few years ago, she worked full-time as well. In fact, Aunt Irene only recently retired after working for over forty years at various garment factories. And the only reason she quit at that point was because she had no choice when McCoy's Manufacturing Plant finally closed.

Aunt Irene has an incredible work ethic. I can still picture her kitchen, lined with several freezers; each called a "deep freeze," filled to the brim with frozen peas, dried apples, corn, okra, and homemade desserts. Of course, she, like the rest of the women I knew, prepared this all herself and grew every bit of it in her own garden. Aunt Irene, like many of steel magnolias in our area, always had more than one garden. Aunt Irene not only has a strong work ethic, she has a strong spirit. Her life certainly has not been easy. Her only son passed away several years ago, while only in his forties. And her husband, my Uncle Lester, died years earlier. She has also recently lost her second husband to a debilitating disease. In spite of all that she'd been through, Aunt Irene has chosen to count her blessings and to be thankful for what she has: her grandchildren, her garden, and her Sunday school class.

And her Sunday school class has been her pride and joy for over four decades. Aunt Irene was recently awarded a pin for forty-seven years of perfect attendance, teaching Sunday school every Sunday morning at the First Baptist Church in Sulligent. I find that fact amazing. To put this in perspective, I did the math; she has taught more than 2, 444 Sunday school lessons to first and second graders, without missing the first Sunday. Not many folks can top that one.

This list of women who possess a strong work ethic would not be complete without the mention of Laura and her mother Mrs. Maggie. Laura currently cares for a garden (at least an acre in size), cans and freezes enough vegetables to feed a small country, maintains an immaculate house that's cleaner than most hospitals, and somehow finds time to prepare for her role as a Sunday school teacher each week. Laura came by this work ethic honestly. Her mother, Mrs. Maggie, worked at Detroit Slacks for approximately forty-five years, managed to raise four wonderful daughters, maintained an enormous garden, grew magnificent flowers, designed quilts and clothing for her family with exquisite detail, and still cooked enough food each day, all from scratch, to feed an entire army.

To say that these women were tough and had a strong work ethic would certainly be an understatement. You rarely ever found these ladies sitting around idle. If they did ever sit down, you could count on the fact that they'd have a pan of beans in their laps to shell or perhaps a shirt to mend. And whenever you drove up into their yards, you learned to never be surprised at what you'd find them doing. Most of the time, you'd find them with their hands wrapped around a garden hoe all bent over as they chopped away at the johnson grass that managed to find its way into their gardens or you'd find them outside burning a pile of leaves and sticks. I've yet to figure out the purpose in this practice; perhaps our mothers were secretly pyromaniacs.

The women I grew up with were tough pioneer types who could hold their own in most any circumstance. In my opinion, Jake described them best when he said, "Although these women looked like ladies, they could bite the head off a nail." They were, without a doubt, distinctly feminine, like Southern magnolias, yet at the same time unbelievably strong, like they were somehow crafted from steel.

Three-Acre Gardens

Gardens in our area were massive vegetable gardens whose area was measured in square acres, not square feet. Anything less than an acre was considered a hobby or something to be pitied. These were some serious gardens. And ours did not contain the first flower.

Most of our mothers never had time for a rose garden or any other flower garden for that matter. What we needed was something practical, something to provide for our basic need for food. And since we had a garden that was larger than most city blocks, food was the one thing we always had plenty of. Like others in our community, we planted just about every vegetable and fruit that would grow in a Southern climate. Each year we'd plant corn, okra, squash, peppers, sweet potatoes, onions, carrots, cucumbers, cabbage, turnip greens, radishes, mustard greens, butterbeans, tomatoes, watermelons, pumpkins, green beans, black-eyed peas, and my least favorite, purple hulls. Unlike people who grew up in cities and suburbs and selected their produce along the aisles of Food World, we selected our produce along the garden rows behind our homes. Thus, the once a week trip to the grocery store was merely a way to obtain a few staples such as eggs, bacon, sausage, buttermilk, sweet milk, flour, cornmeal, and sugar as well as a few occasional soft drinks and snacks. So, with the exception of a few store-bought items, the garden was our livelihood, and due to its size and variety, provided us with enough fruits and vegetables to feed the entire population of Detroit, Alabama.

Due to the enormous size of the gardens in our area, much of what was grown was often given away. I will never forget how Mr. Roy, who maintained a garden spanning several acres well in to his eighties, would generously give our family and several other families in the town paper bags filled to the brim with sweet scuppernongs, luscious red tomatoes, fresh cucumbers, and all sorts of peas and countless other vegetables. Mr. Roy had a heart of gold and intentionally planted more than his family could possibly consume in order that he might share his abundance with others in our community.

In rural Alabama, this act of sharing was quite common. Our family might give away a bushel of purple hull peas from the garden; in turn, someone else would give us several sacks full of okra. Aunt Irene, who at 77 still maintains a three-acre garden, was notorious for giving away more than her family could ever conceive of consuming. But, to be honest, my brother Willy and I dreaded seeing Aunt Irene drive up with those plastic containers full of vegetables since we knew we'd be spending the better part of the next few days preparing these for mom to can in the trusty pressure cooker.

We were expected to not only prepare things for the pressure cooker but to also work alongside our parents by picking this produce right out of the garden. We youngsters never thought we were quite cut out for this. We enjoyed being outside, but we did not like the piercing sting of okra on our skin, the sweat that would form on our foreheads and drip down into our eyes like rain, the feel of knife blades across our ankles as we walked through the johnson grass, or the itching sensations created by annoying insects. And since our gardens were over an acre in size, this job could take hours.

We spent hours, not only in our own gardens, but in the gardens of our neighbors as well. We'd carry around plastic five-gallon buckets to our neighbor's pea patch at the break of dawn and maneuver, just so, through the plants still laden with dew.

When I worked in our own garden, which was more often than I'd have liked, I did try to position myself so I'd have the task of pulling the corn from the stalk. At least I could stand up and do this. It certainly beat walking around all bent over picking butterbeans or purple hull peas. The only thing worse, in my opinion, was cutting okra off the stalk. This stinging sensation would penetrate deep into your skin and felt much like fiberglass insulation.

Not only were we expected to help with the collection of the vegetables in the hot humid weather, we were expected to assist with the shelling of the peas, shucking of the corn, and snapping of the green beans. This was slightly more bearable since we would at least be allowed to do these tasks inside, in front of the television, and most importantly, near a fan. I will never forget how the beans, peas, and corn were brought into the house in plastic bushel containers, the size of five-gallon paint buckets. We'd be trapped in the middle of the room surrounded by a fortress of vegetables, for what seemed like eternity.

After each vegetable was shelled, shucked, or snapped, our mothers would spend numerous hours canning with pressure cookers and freezing the home-grown vegetables. In small-town Alabama, it was never a matter of whether or not you owned a freezer or pressure cooker; it was a matter of how many your family actually owned. Our family owned only one "deep freeze" and only one pressure cooker, but the Cash family owned at least two full-sized freezers, each at least six feet in length, in addition to their two refrigerator freezers. Aunt Irene, at last count, held the record number of full-size deep freezers: She owns five.

At the end of each summer, every freezer would be filled to its capacity with packs of vegetables, blackberries, and dried apples sealed in plastic bags, and every kitchen cabinet would be lined with row after row of Mason jars filled with garden-grown vegetables, preserved and tightly sealed with metal lids. With this stockpile of food, there would be no chance of hunger during the upcoming months.

The only problem was that the can goods in our house were always a little frightening. Mother-bless her heart-was an abstract-random sort of person and would often neglect to label the lid with the date. Usually, it was just a guessing game as to the expiration date. We usually shook the jar around, inspected its contents carefully, peeled back the rubber coating of the lid to take a sniff, and hoped for the best.

As my friends and I have reflected on this time, we've had to admit that we're actually thankful for our gardening experiences. Although we did not realize it at the time, we learned several lessons. From these experiences, we developed the following: a strong work ethic, a sense of accomplishment, a philosophy that anything worth doing is worth doing well, an appreciation for the land, and a sense of responsibility for our families as well as our neighbor.

◆   ◆   ◆

Maybe one day when I retire, I'll have my own garden; then again, maybe the memories are enough…

Building Blocks

A child's life is like a piece of paper on which every person leaves a mark.
~ Chinese Proverb

Daddy taught me the letters of the alphabet when I was three years old using a set of wooden blocks with individual letters carved into each side. The first letter I could recognize was "H." I still have this particular block. It's priceless and serves as a reminder of how my father valued education.

Although I knew this, I never knew just how much until my Aunt Nellie recently shared with me a conversation between my mother and father, the day before his death.

"We will sell off the land or even the house, whatever it takes, to pay for Tina's college education," he said.

Daddy died the following day, December 30 of 1982, when I was only nineteen and a sophomore at the University of Montevallo. Most of all, I regret the fact he was unable to see this dream fulfilled.

This dream for my education started early. Daddy insisted I attend school as soon as possible and made arrangements for me to attend kindergarten, even before public kindergartens existed in our area. In 1968, Charles Richardson and Daddy took turns driving Elizabeth and me over to the United Methodist Church in Sulligent, which was a ten-mile trip, one way.

Once we arrived at the church, Elizabeth and I proceeded to the basement, where our class met until noon. Here, we'd walk into a room filled with plastic chairs in a rainbow of colors. Elizabeth and I always made it a point to choose matching chairs. At age five, making sure that you had matching chairs was high on the priority list.

I also remember Choice Time. During this interval of time, we could choose to paint, to build blocks, to look at books, or to role-play in the toy kitchen. Although I do remember playing in these centers, one thing stands out: getting into trouble during Choice Time. Originally, I'd told my teacher I wanted to paint during this interval of time. Then, I did the unthinkable. I changed my mind. I decided I'd rather play with the blocks. Turned out, once you'd made your choice, you no longer had the choice to change. I received a lecture that day and tried from that day forward to be more reflective before I voiced my final decision.

Following Choice Time, our teacher would ask us to arrange our plastic chairs in a semicircle, in order that she might read us a book or two. Once our teacher had finished reading to us, we would often rearrange our chairs to form a circle. Then, we'd play musical chairs. We'd slowly walk around, staring at each chair, so we could leap into a seat the moment our teacher lifted the needle off of the record. The object was to find an available seat among the few chairs left in the circle. No one wanted to be left standing.

As noon approached, our teacher would lead us in some type of musical activity. I remember our teacher placing a vinyl 45 RPM on the turntable of our record player and encouraging us to shake little tambourines and maracas to the beat of various songs and dance around the room. Following music time, we would collect our belongings and prepare to return home.

On the way home, I would count the five bridges we would cross on Highway 17 as we made the ten-mile journey and would discuss all the things I'd learned that day.

As we made our journey home, Daddy just smiled.

Reading, 'Riting, 'Rithmetic, and Red Floor Sweep

Detroit Elementary was similar to many schools yet was certainly different than others. This elementary school was located in the heart of town, along Highway 17, right next door to Mrs. Maggie's. It no longer contains elementary-age children or basal readers, but in recent years has been transformed into a flea market and even a restaurant. Today, all that exists is a mere shell of the building that I once knew. The school closed in August of 1988, once the enrollment of the entire school body dropped below ninety students.

Detroit Elementary once consisted of classes ranging from kindergarten through grade seven. It was where my friends and I were first introduced to the Four R's: reading, 'riting, 'rithmetic, and something which was unique to our school: red floor sweep.

Floor sweep, as we called it, was something that looked like red sawdust, coated in oil. About every three weeks or so, we'd spread this stuff all over the tile floor of our classroom as sort of a magnet to collect the floor's dirt and dust. The reason why we students were given this responsibility is quite simple. Our elementary school was part of the Alabama Public School System, with little funding. Therefore, custodial help was a luxury the system could not afford.

Actually, we secretly liked serving as the school's custodians. Putting down floor sweep meant that the entire class would have to put away the textbooks and move our desks over to one side of the room, while a select few threw the red stuff along the vacant side of the room. After sweeping the piles of sawdust and bits of paper into a dustpan, the desks would be promptly moved to the recently cleaned side and the whole process would be repeated with the red sawdust thrown to the opposite side of the room. Once both sides of the room were clean, the red sawdust was carefully placed into a plastic bucket, to be recycled and used again in a few weeks.

Since we didn't have a janitor employed at our school, we spent a considerable amount of time, out of class, doing odd services such as using the industrial strength electric buffer to shine the hall floors. I can still picture Willy and Jake holding onto the handles of the buffer, peeking over the top of the thing since they were only four feet tall at the time, and maneuvering it in a snake-like fashion down the middle of the school's hall, like inexperienced employees holding onto a jackhammer. And I can still picture a few of us emptying the metal garbage cans, dusting the chalkboard erasers by pounding them on the walls of the brick building, and running the snack store.

Being in charge of the snack store was a real honor. It was a job reserved for a select few. You had to be able to count money and figure change. This, by the way, was before the days of digital cash registers. We had to do mental math. The snack store was located in a small room, about the size of a closet, near the foyer and had a window with glass slats that resembled window blinds, which rolled outward as you turned the crank. This small room was stocked with a smorgasbord of candy bars, crackers, and chips. For a dime, you could buy yourself a bag of chips or some peanut butter crackers that we called "Nabs." Across the hall from the snack store was the drink machine equipped with glass bottles and a built-in bottle opener where fifteen cents could buy you any soft drink of your choice.

Detroit Elementary was designed in a multi-age fashion with two grades in each classroom. Ironically, many of today's classrooms are now designed in this manner; educators currently call this multi-age concept "progressive." Detroit, Alabama was obviously way ahead of its time.

Actually, attending a small rural school such as Detroit Elementary had its advantages. As first graders, we were able to listen in on the second grade lessons and thus learned this information a year ahead of time. The same was true the following year when we were promoted to Mrs. Livingston's second and third grade class. Here we memorized our multiplication tables in the second grade as we listened to the third graders recite these on a regular basis. Another advantage we had at Detroit Elementary was the size of our classes. There were only six people in my particular grade; so to say that we received individualized attention was quite an understatement. And since our teachers taught us for two consecutive years, they knew our strengths and our weaknesses, inside and out.

On the other hand, there were a few disadvantages. For one, Detroit Elementary did not have its own library, at the time. Instead, we had the Book Mobile. Each week a white van, basically a library on wheels, would drive up into our school's parking lot. We'd each be given a certain length of time to examine the Book Mobile's contents; our book selections would then be placed in a black plastic box that resembled something like a recycling bin. The process would be repeated on a weekly basis as we returned the borrowed books and selected new ones. Grace, as I remember, was always the most excited about the arrival of the Book Mobile. Unlike most of her peers, Grace was a voracious reader. While most of her classmates (myself included) were content to merely read the third grade SRA cards, Grace was busy reading any classic she could get her hands on.

Other memories of my elementary years are still lodged in my mind, like impressions made in fresh cement. I can still picture the first day of school on the playground when Grace asked if she could sit down in the swing next to me. I can still picture the wooden geometric solids, located in the back of Mrs. Virginia Mae Alexander's first and second grade classroom as well as the SRA reading kit filled with its short stories on color-coded cards. I can still picture the reading circle located at the front of the classroom with green plastic chairs lining its circumference. I can still picture our first reading books with stories about children named Dick, Jane, and Sally. I can still picture the thick avocado green (it was the late 60s) curtains that covered the windows and lined one entire wall of the room. I can still picture the aluminum Christmas tree positioned in the front of the classroom, adorned with red satin balls. I can also still picture the portraits of George Washington and Abraham Lincoln that hung over the chalkboard and glared down at each of us as we learned our alphabet and addition facts as well as a little history about our nation.

I can still picture our fourth and fifth grade classroom and can still remember working with Jessica, Lori, and Grace on a book depicting each U.S. president. I remember standing before our class and reciting the Gettysburg Address, the U.S. presidents, and the capitals of all fifty states. I can remember watching filmstrips, which were displayed on a white screen and projected from a small piece of equipment. This piece of equipment had a handle on the side, which had to be manually turned in order to advance the next slide. Along with the filmstrip was a record player, which provided the audio as well as a beep sound to signal the advancement of the next slide. This, of course, was years before the VCR.

I can still recall the days in this class when Jessica, Lori, Grace, and I would routinely push our desks together during snack time and combine all our chips and cookies into one big smorgasbord of snacks. And I'll certainly never forget the day that one of our classmates, who was always prone to allergies, sneezed and sprayed a fine nasal mist all over our perfect mound of food, just as we were about to indulge. It's funny...the things we remember.

I can still picture the look on my third grade teacher's face when I brought a live blue jay to share with my third grade class. I vividly recall that my bird was more mobile than I'd anticipated. While we were seated in a circle reading from our trusty basal texts, in a round robin fashion, the blue jay I'd brought to share decided to pop out of his shoebox. He proceeded to hop around the aisles of our classroom, leaving behind a distinctive trail that I later was forced to clean. The blue jay, which I'd brought for *Show and Tell*, showed more than I'd bargained for that day.

I can still picture our sixth- and seventh-grade classroom and our teacher, who also served as our school's principal. This was one teacher who believed in running a tight ship. I can still hear her fingers snapping as she reprimanded those who had strayed off the straight and narrow path. I can also picture the thick gray folding curtain, which resembled a massive accordion, located in the back of her classroom. This curtain served as a room divider between our class and the cafeteria. And I can remember how we would send secret notes to our friends by sliding these letters underneath the Iron Curtain, as we called it. Much to our dismay, our teacher had a keen nose for mischief and would quickly sniff out any wrong doings. Thus, our communication underneath the Iron Curtain was somewhat of a rarity and was often intercepted.

I can also picture the playground, equipped with two sets of swings on long chains attached to metal poles, a slide with a ladder about five feet in length, a couple of wooden seesaws, and a merry-go-round with a wooden base. When we were in first, second, and third grades, our recess time was spent here playing make-believe, sliding down the short metal slide, taking turns pushing each other around the merry-go-round, and seeing who could swing high enough to touch the limbs on the trees. Afternoons were spent playing chase and designing houses out of the pine straw that covered the playground like brown shag carpet. We were all equal, so to speak, at this age, but that all changed once we were promoted to fourth grade and expected to play competitively on the softball and kickball field. The softball field was located directly behind the school. This is where I first discovered that I was no athlete. Although Grace and I could hold our own in the classroom, this was not the case when we stepped out onto the field. We were athletically challenged. No one wanted us on his or her team. We were considered liabilities. Whenever the class was divided into teams, the same two people were always left standing, waiting to be chosen. Each week, the words of the chosen captains were the same and are now forever branded in my mind:

"I suppose I'll take Tina for my team, if you'll agree to take Grace."

It doesn't take a rocket scientist to figure out that Grace and I were at the bottom of the athletic taxonomy. While many of our peers could effortlessly hit the ball fifty yards or so into the trees surrounding our field, Grace and I did well to have the bat even make contact with the ball. Of course, we coped by pretending like sports didn't matter and by volunteering to stay inside and help our teachers grade papers while our peers enthusiastically played softball and kickball on the field behind our school.

Other memories of Detroit Elementary are still quite vivid. I can still picture the day our fourth- and fifth-grade teacher flipped over in his wooden chair, causing his brown shoes to point upward, like arrows, to the florescent lights. And I remember the day Grace and Keith were crowned Detroit Elementary's Halloween Queen and King. I can still picture the day that Mother took Willy home with a bleeding forehead from injuries he'd sustained during a playful pillow fight with Jake during naptime and how Jake cried for the remainder of the day. I still remember the day in first grade when Sarah told me about Santa and the day Mrs. Alexander bragged on my reading skills.

Looking back, I now realize we were fortunate to attend Detroit Elementary. We received individualized instruction. We were provided with many opportunities to serve as leaders. We were taught to take pride in our school and country. We were taught the meaning of having a work ethic. And most importantly, Mrs. Alexander, our first grade teacher, instilled in us the importance of embracing imagination and wonder. I'm trying each day to take her advice.

Snapshots of High School

My high school memories are like random snapshots that have been pasted together to form a collage. Most of these photos depict simple ordinary days. No one photo really stands out. Rather, these snapshots blend together and overlap, making it difficult to discern where one event begins and another ends.

As I visualize this collage of memories, I see snapshots of my closest friends Grace, Theresa, Susan, Jane, Ruth, Jessica, Daniel, William, and Ralph. In these snapshots, I see candid pictures of times spent together in trigonometry, geometry, physics, biology, and chemistry classes. I can picture our class as we practiced conversational Spanish and performed some of Shakespeare's plays. I see moments spent stuffing toilet paper into chicken wire to form floats for our small-town parades and dressing up in funny costumes in order to be initiated into the Beta Club. I see us dissecting frogs, using the Bunsen burner in chemistry class, learning to maneuver between orange cones in Drivers Ed, attending pep rallies, participating in beauty pageants, riding on cars during Homecoming parades, cheering during football and basketball games, going out on double dates, riding around town after cheerleading practice, and dancing at proms.

By many accounts, my memories may be much like those of just about any former high school student in America. On the other hand, there were some differences...

For one, since our school's k-12 enrollment was around 1,000, and our particular class was made up of a mere fifty-five students, competition wasn't really an issue. If you wanted to serve on the student council, act as class president, be a member of the cheerleading squad, or serve on the scholastic team, odds were in your favor.

Proms were also quite different. Rather than a gym or hotel ballroom, our proms were held in our school's cafeteria, which we decorated with inexpensive crepe paper and balloons. Entertainment was usually a local radio disc jockey as opposed to a popular band. And we drove to proms in cars and trucks; limousines were out of the question.

Another difference at SHS was that guys drove to school during deer hunting season with firearms mounted in their truck's gun racks. I'm not condoning this practice…just stating a fact.

Class trips were few and far between. To us, just traveling a couple of hours to Birmingham to attend the Beta Club Convention was a big deal.

And the mode of transportation was certainly unique since Lamar County did not exactly have the tax base to charter a bus. Thus, we were transported to the Beta Club Convention in a school bus…painted white…with the word "SPECIAL" stenciled in bold black letters across the front.

I am not making this up.

And while I must admit that I have few memories of what we actually learned from an academic standpoint at the Beta Club Convention, I do remember a few things. I remember how much we enjoyed the company of our English/Spanish teacher, who was brave enough to take our group to Birmingham. And I remember shaving cream wars…which took place long after our chaperones had checked on us for the night.

My closest friends and I could actually hold our own, when it came to fighting others with shaving cream. I don't remember exactly when, but at some point early on in the game a few of us came up with the idea of simply replacing the shaving cream cap with the top off of our aerosol can of hairspray. This adjustment in equipment enabled us to squirt shaving cream ten or so feet. While our peers fought within close range and took the chance that their weapon would be snatched from their fingertips, Grace and I showered our peers with shaving cream from a distance and fared pretty well.

And when I think back to our infamous shaving cream wars, I remember the night we stayed at a hotel in Birmingham during one of our Beta Club Conventions and decorated the windows outside our balcony with a plethora of white foam. It looked like a blizzard had mysteriously blown into the Deep South. Most of all, I can still picture the expressions of the hotel maids when they discovered our manufactured snow. They were not happy. And I can also hear them yelling all kinds of obscenities about us and can picture them hauling green water hoses up the stairs to the floor of our hotel to spray off the windows and balcony.

For some reason, this snapshot overlaps with the one of our Senior Trip. Perhaps we had a shaving cream war on that trip as well. I honestly don't remember. What I do remember is standing next to a van with my closest friends as we waved good-bye to our families. Since only a few of us from our senior class (eleven, to be exact) wanted to go to Disney World, our chemistry teacher and principal simply loaded us up in a van and took off for Orlando. There were no medical forms or permission slips, just instructions to meet at a certain time armed with some luggage and spending money.

As I think back to this trip, I can still picture our group spending the entire night in Walt Disney's park during Grad Night, visiting with seniors from other areas across the country, riding every roller coaster in the park, and listening to bands. And I can still picture the look on my friends' faces when our chaperones surprised us with a trip to the beaches of St. Augustine.

There are many other random, seemly insignificant memories, which are a part of my collage of thoughts. Included in these are snapshots of how my peers tormented one of our favorite teachers. I can still hear of one of my classmates running by our class on a regular basis and yelling, "The British are coming!" I also remember the day we all decided to turn our desks so they faced the back wall when our teacher entered the room. He counted to twenty. At ten, we turned our desks 180 degrees. When he got to twenty, we turned our desks to the front. I can also hear the "Beep!" sound some of my peers would interject when our teacher would show us a filmstrip. Not being able to discern the difference in the sounds, the timing would be off causing him to finish the filmstrip long before the film's audio ended.

Other random memories that are still a part of me include being spun around on the shoulders of guys in a game called "helicopter," finding dissected frog legs in my locker, going skating in Hamilton with our senior class and high school principal, watching our math teacher perform magic as she somehow made trigonometry meaningful, dressing up for initiation into the Spanish Club, and making banners out of butcher paper for basketball games. I also remember riding around Vernon in Susan's white Trans Am, attending mud derbies, driving fifty miles to the mall in Columbus, sharing secrets during slumber parties at Theresa's, going to Halloween parties at Susan's, riding by the houses of guys we secretly had crushes on, building pyramids as a cheerleader, driving down roller coaster hill in Hamilton, ringing in the 80s during New Year's Eve, and visiting the campus of The University of Alabama with my closest friends.

This collage is made up of moments spent sharing dreams, secrets, doubts, and sorrows. It's made up of both laughter and tears. Most importantly, it's made up of time spent with friends, forming bonds that have only strengthened through the years.

Television

Out in the country, cable was not an option; this luxury was only available to the privileged few, who lived within the city limits of Detroit. Even if we'd had access to cable lines out where we lived, my parents would have definitely vetoed the idea. Cable was considered an extra and clearly something we could not afford. So we grew up watching the programs that our trusty television antenna could transmit. This included two channels, four and nine, which broadcast the networks of CBS and NBC. On a good night, when a satellite was positioned in precisely the right place, we could also pick up PBS and on rare occasions, even ABC. Thus, some classics like *Leave it to Beaver* and *The Munsters*, which were televised on ABC, were rarely a part of our viewing repertoire.

I don't think we missed all that much. Although at the time, the mystery of what we were being deprived of made us beg for a satellite dish. Of course, this wasn't a real need, like food or clothing, so this idea was quickly dismissed. The closest thing we ever had was this plastic rotary dial, attached to a metal base about the size of a phone book, which actually rotated our outdoor antenna. It made this humming sound, sort of like an alien spacecraft, when we turned the dial. We thought we really had something. With the rotary dial, we could only pick up a few channels, but at least we didn't have to go outside, wrap our arms around the fifteen-foot antenna pole, twist it manually, and yell from the window.

"Is that any better?"

In turn the person assigned to watch the television screen would usually yell back, "No, try the other direction!"

"What about now?"

"Try turning it the other way."

"What'd you say?"

"I said turn it the other way!"

"How does it look now?"

"That'll have to do, I guess."

Now, as an adult with digital satellite and cable television, I can choose from over 100 television shows with the simple click of the remote. I now realize…we did not miss a thing.

The Media

Our parents listened to WERH, a local radio station which broadcast from Hamilton, a town about fifteen miles away with a population of around 6,000. WERH was located at 970 on the AM dial and was known for its country and Southern gospel music. This station provided farm reports each day at noon as well as weather and the latest news. WERH was most famous for a special program called *In Memoriam*, which was broadcast at ten o'clock sharp, each morning.

This special program announced all the names of the recently deceased as well as the funeral arrangements. And whenever this program was put on the air, many of the citizens of our area stopped everything and listened in complete silence. If we ran into the room at around ten o'clock, our parents would hold up an index finger over their mouths.

"Hush! It's time for *In Memoriam!*"

Our parents and grandparents had to make sure that no one they knew had died without their knowledge. I can't recall if they ever heard a name announced that they didn't already know about, since word traveled faster than the speed of light around our area, but they listened nonetheless, religiously, Monday through Saturday, at exactly ten o'clock. And just to make sure all the listeners caught every detail of each funeral arrangement, the station repeated the listing of those in our area that were "lying in state."

The funny thing about this program was that right before *In Memoriam* started, the announcer would say, "*In Memoriam* is brought to you today by our local corn syrup." That just seemed like a strange sponsor for death announcements.

Other unique broadcasts from WERH were the blasting sounds of a fire engine whenever the volunteer fire department was called to a fire and something called *Bulletin Board*. This was a fifteen-minute session where people could call in to the radio station to buy or sell personal items. It was our own version of eBay.

We were also kept apprised of news by information published in weekly editions of *The Lamar Democrat* and the *Lamar Leader*, which contained world news as well local information. You never knew what you'd find on the front page though. There were many accounts of men holding up long snakes they'd killed or displaying tomatoes they'd grown that were as big as pumpkins. And there were community gossip sections in the paper as well. Mrs. Millie, bless her heart, wrote the *Detroit Doings* section when we were growing up. As she made her rounds selling Avon to our mothers, she'd take notes related to our active social lives, which in our case only involved trips to Wal-Mart or perhaps to Mrs. Maggie's house for Sunday dinner. It never mattered though. Just about anything we did was considered news and was therefore worthy of publication. And that's the real charm of a small Southern town.

Trick-or-Treat

Trick-or-treating out in the country was certainly different from what children experienced in the suburbs. Since the closest neighbor we had was at least a half-mile away, there was no way that we could walk from house-to-house. I can just picture us trying to keep up with each other as we ran a six-mile marathon from door-to-door, crawling up to the neighbors' front doors, trying to catch our breath and forming the infamous words, "Trick or Treat!" Luckily for us, this wasn't necessary. Our parents gladly volunteered to drive us from house-to-house as we slowly filled our sacks to the brim with individually wrapped pieces of candy, with popcorn balls wrapped in cellophane, and with gooey caramel apples.

On Halloween night, we never had to worry about our parents dropping us off in the middle of a subdivision to wander around aimlessly among strangers. We didn't have subdivisions or strangers, for that matter. We knew every family within a thirty-mile radius of our home.

Sometimes this lack of anonymity could pose a problem. When we drove up into our neighbors' yards, people could easily identify our car. This caused many of the ladies to instantly recognize us, despite our costumes.

"Oh, look at Tina and little Willy. Aren't they cute?"

Since they knew us well, they also wanted to talk to us. Of course, this was the last thing on our minds, since we wanted to visit as many houses as possible during the one night of the year when candy was being given away by the handfuls. But we were instructed to be polite and to take the time to talk as long as they wanted. And we did talk at length one Halloween night when we rang Mrs. Smith's doorbell. Being an elderly lady, she misread our intentions and thought we were just coming over for a visit. She obviously had no idea what night it was. Before long, I found myself sitting on her Queen Anne sofa all dressed up in a witch suit, along with Willy disguised as Casper the ghost, and trying to make conversation for what seemed like an eternity. We left without the first piece of candy. I suppose our costumes didn't offer the first clue.

Our costumes were, for the most part, homemade. Mother would usually donate a couple of old white tattered sheets, which had seen better days, to our cause. These would be magically transformed with the help of some stainless-steel scissors into ghost costumes. We were quite original. On one occasion, I even wound some dog chains around my waist for an added effect.

On a few rare occasions, we would talk our parents into purchasing those plastic facemasks with the frail rubber bands tied around the back that would inevitably break in half, early in the night. After trying to retie the rubber bands around our heads, the crazy things would no longer fit, and so we'd often just give up and end up holding the masks to our faces with one hand while we held onto our bag of goodies with the other. Before we went trick-or-treating, Willy and I would often dress up in our own costumes and attempt to scare others as they drove up into the yard. We'd hide behind the corner of our house until we heard the car doors slam. As the trick-or-treaters approached the front door, we'd rush out from behind our hiding place and do our best to catch them off guard and simply scare them, but like many of my former plans, this one backfired.

I had planned to be a ghost that year. Since I was only about four feet tall at the time, the long white sheet pooled around the ground with extra material wadded around my ankles. I didn't realize this would be a problem. It was. That year, as I ran around from behind the corner yelling and flinging my arms in the air, I tripped on the sheet, right in front of our trick-or-treaters. I can still picture the look of horror on their faces as they watched me fall like a tree, face down, onto the hard ground. As I wallowed around like a pig in a poke, all tangled up in the sheet with dog chains, trying to figure out a way to get back on my feet, the group came over and stared down at me.

"Hey kid. Are you all right?"

I was fine, unless you count my bruised ego. This, of course, wasn't my last encounter with being graceful, but I've decided to keep some of those stories to myself…

Christmas in the Deep South

Christmas time in the rural South resembled the festive traditions that many others experienced across the nation, with a few exceptions.

For one, families in rural areas rarely purchased their trees at a Christmas tree farm. Instead, families simply located a Christmas tree on their own land, chopped it down, and brought it into the house for decorating.

I recall selecting a tree each year by walking around our forty acres in search of a cedar with some degree of symmetry. And I remember helping my family drag the chosen tree into the house, watching my daddy saw away at the tree's base, and mounting the Christmas tree in a simple metal stand. I also remember helping Willy decorate our evergreen with multi-colored bulbs, cheap silver garland, and hand-painted glass ornaments.

I also remember the year we somehow talked my parents into actually buying us an aluminum Christmas tree. At the time, it was the latest rage; so we wanted to have one of our very own. It came with a silver pole, with holes drilled in specific places to hold the aluminum branches. I remember inserting each aluminum branch into its own section and standing back to see if it resembled a real tree. I also remember decorating the aluminum tree with Christmas balls wrapped with red satin thread. After all of the ornaments were in place and the tree was centered in the window, we would then plug in our rotating color wheel. This plastic wheel was made up of four sections, each different in color, and was mounted like a globe to a light source. Once it was plugged into the electrical socket, it would slowly spin around and disseminate rays of blue, orange, green, and red onto the aluminum branches.

Although families in Detroit, Alabama, displayed aluminum trees in the 60s and 70s like others from across the nation, Christmas in the Deep South was different. One of the main differences was that snow rarely fell from the sky. It had to be created from cotton batting, from plastic flakes in a bag, or from a can of snow spray. Since snow was such a rarity, we never owned a snowbrush or a sled. Instead, on the rare occasion when it did snow, we would walk up to the highest point of a hill and would sit down inside one of Mother's galvanized metal tubs. We would then push ourselves off the top of the hill while seated in the metal tub and would hold onto the tub's handles for dear life as we slid down the hills surrounding our home.

Other heartwarming memories I have of Christmas include playing the role of Mary in our church's program, watching Willy, Jake, and Mark walk down the church's aisle dressed as shepherds, listening to the congregation sing various Christmas carols, and checking our red stockings on Christmas morning for gifts from Santa.

I hope I'll always be able to recall these memories and will be able to picture Daddy's enthusiasm as he opened the simple presents we gave him, Mother cooking Christmas dinner, and Willy waking me up at five o'clock on Christmas morning to unwrap our gifts from Santa. Perhaps in writing these simple yet cherished accounts I'll always be able to picture what the holidays were like as a child…when Christmas was magical.

Law Enforcement

Law enforcement in Detroit, Alabama is somewhat different from other areas. Detroit has not employed a policeman in decades. This Detroit doesn't need one. Here, people simply police themselves. And for the most part, folks feel relatively safe. Mayberry springs to mind, except for the fact that it doesn't have a deputy or even a town sheriff for that matter. It's the sort of place where residents would not think twice about leaving their car keys in the ignition when parked outside the grocery store, bank, post office, or church. Growing up, I can never recall locking my car doors. Most of the time, we just parked our cars in the driveway, with keys left in the ignition. The only time we even considered locking our houses was at night, and like most folks in this area, we often forgot to bother with it at all.

Someone once asked me what we did when we experienced problems since there were no policemen within ten miles of our hometown. I simply replied, "I don't recall anyone ever having any problems." The only exception I can think of is the time someone from out-of-town tried to rob our bank...

A few years ago, a man walked into the First National Bank with the intention of robbing the local branch. He had no idea what was in store for him. When he entered the bank with his gun, he was met by a wall of bulletproof glass about an inch thick that ran from the top of the ceiling down to the teller's window. Flustered, the robber stood motionless with his loaded gun, while the tellers, who were clearly protected behind a fortress of glass, made strange faces at him. I suppose he figured he could hold a customer for ransom, but there were no customers. Realizing what a predicament he was in, he turned to escape through the front door and down into the woods behind the bank, but the men in this area, who could toss around fifty-pound bales of hay like matchsticks, apprehended him in no time.

He was easy to spot. He stood out like a sore thumb...as the only stranger in town.

Behind the Wheel

Driving in the Detroit, Alabama was quite different from what residents experienced in cities and suburbs. Residents of this Detroit never had to worry about dealing with annoying traffic, parking decks or even traffic lights. Drivers never waited in a traffic jam or worried about missing an exit. And they certainly didn't worry about road rage, since one could travel for miles before encountering another car. The main thing a driver had to worry about was dodging deer along the blacktop.

Since Clint, Jessica, and Jake grew up on a farm, they got in some driving experience early, much earlier than the rest of us. In fact, by the time they were in first grade, they were driving most of the trucks and tractors around the soybean and cotton fields on a regular basis. This was understandably a surprise to those who were from out-of-town.

On one occasion, one of Jessica's relatives (named Walter) came over to sit a spell with Mr. Roy. After finishing a glass of sweet tea and a piece of Mrs. Belle's blackberry cobbler, it came time for Walter to go back to Laura and Ken's house, so he sauntered up to the pickup truck and scanned the area looking for an adult.

"Who's going to drive me back over to Ken's?"

"I am," replied a confident Jessica, dangling the truck's keys high in the air.

"But you're only seven years old," replied Walter.

"Well, she *always* drives," said five-year old Jake as he shrugged his shoulders and hopped up into the truck, like riding with a seven-year old behind the wheel was no big deal.

A few years later, when Jake was first learning to drive the family's farm equipment, Ken gave him explicit instructions as to the route to take. Jake was to drive Ken's truck with the attached water trailer over to a certain site, fill the containers with water, and then make a U-turn back. Once Ken was out of sight, Jake gave Willy a cockeyed smile and said, "I've got a better idea."

Jake's plan was to drive directly toward the site and then put the truck in reverse to simply back straight out; however, with a water trailer hitched to the back of the truck, maneuvering the equipment turned out to be much more cumbersome than he'd anticipated. Jake tried again and again to back up the truck. His plan wasn't working.

Ken momentarily looked up from his tractor and noticed what Jake was attempting to do. Minutes later, Jake and Willy glanced over the rows of soybeans, only to see Ken rapidly approaching on his tractor.

Jake whispered, "Uh-oh."

Due to the relatively flat terrain, the guys could see for miles. They watched as Ken's tractor gathered speed along the horizon. Each time Ken pressed the tractor's accelerator, a cloud of black smoke was emitted. It was as if Willy and Jake could see death approaching.

Ken pulled up beside the guys and immediately bounded down from the tractor with his 6'4" ominous frame landing on the hard soil. Jake scrambled out of the truck, knowing that he was in the doghouse for refusing to follow his father's directions. Jake then choked on his words as he attempted to explain his side of the story.

"Daddy, I just thought it would be better to back the trailer in, instead of making a U-turn."

Ken stared down at Jake as he gripped his son's shoulder and said, "Boy, next time I tell you to do something, you'd better do it. You understand?"

Jake looked down at the ground, kicked around some dirt, and quietly whispered, "Yes, Sir." From then on, Jake followed his father's directions to the letter.

Although Clint, Jessica, and Jake were able to drive by the time they were in second grade, this was not the case around our household. Daddy didn't share in this early driving philosophy. He was notorious for his rule-based philosophy and was adamant that Willy and I wait until the very day we turned fifteen and were issued our driving permits. Daddy always did things by the book. When I think back to the days when I was first learning to drive, I can recall how Daddy would always model for us how to drive correctly. I recall how he would say, "When you approach the speed limit sign, you must be going that exact speed when you cross the sign, and when you make a right turn you must form a perfect right angle."

Unfortunately, Daddy's philosophy brushed over me like skimming a rock across water. I didn't take to this legalistic mentality. I remember one occasion when I was first learning to drive. Daddy always insisted on sitting in the middle of the front seat, right beside me, since I only had my driver's permit at the time. This, of course, irritated me to no end, so I decided I'd add a little excitement to our drive home from church one night. As I approached a curve that was more like a semicircle, I rounded it without the slightest loss in acceleration. Daddy, who was always known for his calm demeanor, grabbed the dash of the LTD and with eyes as big as saucers looked straight ahead and yelled, "Good night alive! She's going to kill us all!"

I'm embarrassed to admit that I didn't always drive the speed limit. And, at the age of fifteen I didn't fully comprehend the laws of physics and what the consequences could be. Although, I must admit, it was somewhat difficult driving the speed limit of 55 mph in the LTD. Our family's 1973 LTD was an eight-cylinder model with a 450-motor. I'm not exactly sure what this means, technically speaking; I only know that you simply touched the gas petal and the speedometer would rapidly move across the dial to a three-digit number.

Daddy solved this problem though. When I turned sixteen, he purchased a Ford Fairmont for me from the Maddox Ford Motor Company dealership in Sulligent. It was a 1978, two-door model with a four-cylinder engine. If you floored the gas pedal, it would slowly creep up to 55 mph, unlike the infamous family LTD with its 450-motor, but it was mine and brand new, so I was proud of it nonetheless. Looking back, I'm certain Daddy chose the four-cylinder Ford Fairmont for a reason; I guess he was more aware of my escapades with the family's LTD than I'd imagined.

In the end, we somehow managed to learn to drive and survived pretty much unscathed from it all thanks to some wide-open country roads and more importantly, to some well-equipped guardian angels, who were always on call 24/7.

Corn Stalks and the Farmers Market

As soon as the landscape begins to change from green to deep shades of russet and gold, Clay and I make a special trip down Highway 72 toward one of the local nurseries to purchase bales of hay and stalks of corn…to use as fall decorations. I'm sure both of my parents are rolling in their graves at the very thought.

In Detroit, Alabama, this was unheard of. You could find all the corn stalks you wanted just lying around in the garden. They were never put on display in the front yard. And you certainly didn't buy them. And hay? Well, I never remember seeing this in anyone's front yard. It was only found in the hay fields or in the barn. Hay certainly wasn't embellished with mums and put on display. It's ironic: what we fed to the cows in Detroit is now considered art in our current subdivision in Athens.

A few miles outside of Athens is a Farmers Market which boasts peaches, okra, tomatoes, squash, apples, corn, strawberries, and cucumbers. Clay and I frequent this market quite often to obtain fresh fruits and vegetables. I'm quite sure that my parents, if they were living, would be aghast at the very thought. You never saw produce sold along the side of the road in Detroit, Alabama. I can just imagine what people in that community would have said had there been such a thing:

"They're selling vegetables along the side of the road?"

"Well, I've never heard of such a thing."

"Reckon who will buy such stuff?"

Based on the economic laws of supply and demand, the concept of the farmers market would not have been a hit in my hometown. Of this, I'm certain.

Our local Farmers Market just outside of Athens also contains a section of foods that have been organically grown, whatever that means. Well, I'm pretty certain the vegetables in our backyards were not grown this way. I can still picture Mother, Laura, and Virginia Mae stuffing an old pair of pantyhose with pesticide dust and sprinkling this all over their gardens to the point where it looked like a ton of flour had been inadvertently dumped from the sky. There's no telling what we've consumed in our lifetime. In fact, when I think about all the pesticides and the amount of salt used in canning vegetables in the trusty pressure cooker, I suppose we'll all be preserved better than ole King Tutankhamen.

I suppose I should plant my own garden, complete with corn stalks so that I can just transfer these to the front yard for display during autumn, but for now I'll just continue to stop at the Farmers Market and pay cash for my vegetables and fall decorations.

It's Comin' up a Cloud

It's coming up a cloud, again. But that's to be expected here in Alabama. And since I now live only about 100 miles from where I grew up, the weather pattern is still pretty much the same. The only difference is the sirens. Here, in Athens, sirens blast with a force that can be heard for miles, signaling that a tornado warning has been issued.

That wasn't the case in Lamar County, Alabama. People here could somehow sense it. We didn't have a Doppler Radar system. Our parents served this purpose.

"It's comin' up a cloud," they'd say.

Then there would be a reference to "straight-line winds," and before we knew it we'd be carted off to our trusty storm cellar to ride out the storm the safest way possible.

I was never particularly fond of the storm cellar. Its dark, damp space was the perfect breeding ground for spiders and crickets and the perfect hiding spot for snakes. Knowing this, Daddy would do a thorough inspection before he'd allow us to enter the cellar. I can still picture him with his flashlight, meticulously examining every inch and cranny of the cellar, like a detective investigating a crime scene, while we stood patiently in the doorway and experienced the pounding rain of the impending storm on our shoulders.

Once we were allowed inside the cellar, Mother would light the trusty kerosene lamp by using the matches stored underneath its glass base. Willy and I would then settle down on the white wooden bench and make the best of the situation by projecting animal shadows onto the block walls of the storm cellar.

Seems like I've spent most of my childhood hanging out in the storm cellar, seeking shelter from thunderstorms and tornadoes in an area where tornado season never seemed to end. And my hometown, for some unknown reason, always seemed to be in the path of an impending storm. That was certainly the case on April 3, 1974, the night Guin, which is only eight miles away from my hometown as the crow flies, was literally blown away by a tornado which was later classified as an F-5. I don't think I'll ever forget that night, since we spent most of it in the storm cellar riding out one storm after another, as one tornado after another ravaged the Southeast.

After that infamous and tragic night, we headed for the storm cellar even more regularly, at the slightest hint of stormy weather. And I soon learned to take my Daddy seriously when he'd look up at the sky and repeat those infamous words: "Looks like it's comin' up a cloud."

The Medicine Cabinet

A current friend of mine, whose name shall remain anonymous, has enough prescription medications to stock her own pharmacy. This was not the case for us, as children growing up in the rural South.

Around our households, with the exception of Mother's prescription blood pressure medicine, the strongest thing we ever had to my knowledge was aspirin. Our parents had a simple philosophy. If you had a cut or scrape, they'd dab red stuff that was later taken off the market because it contained mercury (which probably explains a lot) or some rubbing alcohol on the wound. Stomachaches could be treated with some pink liquid. And if you were really in pain, they'd give you an aspirin or two.

Perhaps this was because Detroit did not have a pharmacy. Perhaps it was because prescription medications were costly. Perhaps it was because they didn't know any better. Or perhaps it was just because our parents believed in toughing it out.

I think it was mainly the latter.

I suppose it's a good thing that our medicine cabinet held only a few items because Willy was notorious for getting into whatever he could find. Once we had to rush him to the nearest hospital, which was twenty miles down the road, when he drank an entire bottle of mineral oil. I can still picture that scene like it was yesterday.

From some strange reason, Willy, who was only two years old at the time, opened the kitchen cabinet doors, hid underneath the sink, and turned a bottle of mineral oil upside down, like a homeless drunk downing his favorite bottle of wine. That's what it looked like to me.

So, at the age of four, I ran into the living room and made an announcement: "Willy's drinking whiskey!"

Mother and Daddy exchanged puzzled glances.

"What'd you say?"

Since the strongest thing we had to drink in our Southern Baptist home was some of Mother's sweet tea, they knew it was something else. So, they took off running toward the kitchen only to find Willy just like I'd left him, all drawn up with his knees next to his chest, drinking in the last drop of mineral oil.

I remember Mother scooping up Willy in her arms and heading for the car. On the twenty-mile journey to Hamilton, I sat in the backseat and watched trees zoom by my window as Daddy made record time in the trusty LTD. I remember thinking that drinking stuff under the sink must be serious business.

When we arrived at the hospital, Willy was carted off to the back to have his stomach pumped, while I sat with Daddy out in the waiting room. I remember looking through the tattered magazines the hospital had lying around and trying to entertain myself while Willy underwent his procedure. Hours later, Willy emerged; his face looked like it had been painted with white paste.

But, to be completely honest, Willy wasn't the only one who sampled the few items we had stored in the medicine cabinet. I specifically remember eating about half of a bottle of baby aspirin when I was about three years old. It tasted like candy to me, so I loved the stuff and filled my mouth full. As I write this story, I can still picture the shocked look on Aunt Bertie Mae's face and can visualize how she placed her hand over her heart when she walked into the room, only to find me holding a bottle of baby aspirin with orange crumbs smeared all over my teeth. Aunt Bert didn't volunteer to keep us much after that.

Since those childhood days, I've had time to reflect on our parents' rather minimalist philosophy. And maybe, just maybe, our parents and grandparents had the right philosophy about medication all along. After all, Mr. Roy lived to be 96. And he only took one pill a day.

Decoration Sunday

Soon after the azaleas blossom and decorate our Southern lawns with a myriad of pink, white, and watermelon-colored flowers, we know it's that time of year again. It's as if the azaleas make an announcement: Decoration Sunday is approaching.

On Decoration Sunday, Southerners turn out to cemeteries, dressed in their Sunday best, to decorate the graves of their loved ones with arrangements of silk flowers. Decoration Day is a specific Sunday each year. Each cemetery has its own designated Sunday, usually between the months of April and June.

Decoration Sunday is a big deal, here in the rural South. It's a day when people gather together to remember their loved ones and to visit with family and friends. It's also the one Sunday out of the year when missing the morning church service is an excused absence.

Although I've attended Decoration Sundays all of my life, the ones I remember most vividly are the ones from my childhood. When I was a child, Daddy would load us up in the family LTD and would take us over to Cooper Cemetery on the Saturday before Decoration Day to clean off the graves and prepare them for new arrangements of silk flowers.

As soon as we drove up to the cemetery, Willy and I would always spot a truckload of fresh white sand, placed under one of the oak trees for families to use on their loved ones' graves. We would often beg Daddy to let us play in the mountain of white sand, but his response always indicated this would be disrespectful. Willy and I didn't think the deceased would mind if we played in this pile of sand but knew better than to push the issue with Daddy.

I can still picture Daddy filling up a small bucket with the white sand and later taking a shovel and carefully spreading this substance along his infant son's grave, creating a perfect mound of white sand. He would then remove the faded plastic arrangement with its weather-worn ribbons and would meticulously brush away each grain of sand from Dwayne's granite tombstone with a small hand-held broom. After placing the faded arrangement into a wire bin along with the other tattered year-old arrangements, Daddy would place the shovel and bucket back into the trunk of the car and would then make the twelve-mile journey home.

On Decoration Sunday, we'd put on our best church clothes (which were usually our Easter outfits in our family's case) and would then situate ourselves in the family car to make our way toward Hamilton to Cooper Cemetery, the site where most of my relatives are now buried. Once we arrived, we'd park along the side of the road, take the floral arrangements from the trunk, and then begin placing the silk flowers on the graves of family members.

We always decorated my brother Dwayne's grave first. His arrangement was usually designed with baby blue flowers, wrapped with ribbons stamped with words written with gold glitter.

Once Dwayne's arrangement was securely in place, we'd place artificial flowers on Grandmother Rye's grave and would then putter about the cemetery, in the heat of the morning, placing plastic and silk flowers on any grave which bore the name of Rye. After each artificial flower was stuck in the ground or mounted on a tombstone, we were allowed to roam about the cemetery and visit with our friends and relatives. Each year, it seemed as though the conversations with our relatives never changed.

"Aren't those just the prettiest flowers you've ever seen?"

"You know, purple was always your grandmother's favorite color."

And of course, our relatives invariably said, "You kids are growing like weeds!"

Following a round of twenty questions about school and anything else they could think of to ask, we would walk around with some of our relatives and would read the names and inscriptions on several of the graves. Our aunts and uncles would take the time to share with us, in detail, how the deceased were somehow related to our family. They also discussed what they knew about each person and the effects they had on the lives of others. Now, as an adult, I now realize how important this information was; I only wish I'd paid more attention.

Attending Decoration Sunday at Cooper Cemetery is one tradition I've continued through the years. Although Mother and Daddy have no knowledge of this fact, I hope others can look at the flowers I place on their graves and know that my parents were loved.

I'm sure that's why we still keep the tradition of Decoration Sunday. We all need to take time to remember.

Childproof Homes

Lots of people my age have hired professionals to come into their homes and childproof their houses for safety reasons. These experts have covered the electrical outlets, attached special hinges to the cabinetry, and installed baby gates at each and every entrance. While I applaud this practice, our houses, I must admit, were never childproofed when we were growing up. I'm not condoning the fact that our homes were not equipped with these preventative measures; it's just that things were different in the 1960s and 1970s, especially around our neck of the woods.

We did things that by today's standards would be considered unheard of. We played inside the metal bin that held Ken's cotton and on top of other farm equipment, every chance we had. We rode motorcycles, four wheelers, and our bicycles without thinking about wearing a helmet and played for hours in the dense woods that surrounded our homes without thinking about snakes or other creatures for that matter.

It's a wonder we lived to tell about our childhood when I think back to some of the things we did…like playing with Willy's tractor. This miniature version of a tractor was about three feet high, was made of metal, and was equipped with a steering wheel (which really worked) and had a seat large enough for one person to sit on. I remember how my brother and I would push this tractor up to the top of a hill that was the length of a football field with what seemed like a 45-degree slope. We'd then hop on the toy tractor and place our tiny hands around the steering wheel. Once we were seated, we'd push the tractor just over the edge of the hill, so gravity could do the rest. We'd hold on for dear life as we used the little steering wheel to dodge trees and fallen limbs that surrounded the floor of the densely packed woods behind our house. And on some occasions, when we were unable to dodge the fallen trees, we would be catapulted into thin air.

Of course, I never clocked our speed, but I would guess that given the slope of the hill, we probably flew down at around twenty-five miles per hour, give or take a few. We always managed to stop, one way or another, at the bottom of the hill right before landing in the creek that flowed along the hill's base.

This infamous creek was one that we swam in often, in spite of the fact that it was probably infested with water moccasins and goodness knows what else. And I can still picture how we would swing from a vine into the creek's waters, without thinking about what the consequences might be.

I'm sure that people reading these accounts might wonder why our parents allowed us to roam freely and unsupervised. The answer is simple. This was the norm. This was what children in our area did. Children played on their parents' land, not within the confines of a privacy fence. Plus, we were allowed to roam freely because, at the time, child abduction was unheard of. Around our part of the state, this term was unthinkable. And so, we played in a carefree manner and survived without any serious injuries.

Well…to be honest…there were a few exceptions. Jake managed to break a few bones after he was thrown from a horse. And I sprained my wrist when Willy pushed me off of the top of our washing machine. Otherwise, we survived pretty much unscathed from it all. As I reflect back on this time, I do have to admit I'm grateful God saw fit to provide us with some well-trained guardian angels because we wouldn't have lived to adulthood without some intervention.

Babysitters

Working mothers have often had little choice but to place their children in large daycare facilities. That was not the case in Detroit, Alabama. There were no daycare facilities, just kind women who opened up their households to take in children, like my brother and myself. Since both of my parents worked full-time when we were youngsters, we were supervised by several of our neighbors.

And some of these memories are etched in my mind like carvings in stone. For instance, I remember walking to Detroit Elementary from the Martins' house along with Paula's five children and several others from our community whom she so graciously agreed to keep. I remember the day Mrs. Martin somehow repaired my second grade school photo that had been damaged in a rainstorm on the way home. And I remember watching the *Looney Tunes* sign off on the Martins' large console television.

I also remember spending time at the Calverts' house with their three children: Scott, Jonathan, and Katie. It's anyone's guess as to why Charlotte agreed to keep us…when I think back to our very first encounter. This infamous meeting took place one afternoon after Mother and Daddy had finished up their workday at Detroit Slacks. That afternoon, while our parents spoke with Charlotte and Roger about the possibility of keeping us before and after school, we played outside the Calvert residence like rambunctious ones, running full throttle. Jonathan, who was only four years old at the time, ran full speed in one direction, while Willy, who was about seven, ran full speed in another. As luck would have it, the two met in a head-on collision when they both rounded one corner of the house at the same moment in time, like opposing trains meeting on the same track. Somehow, in spite of the fact that Jonathan entered the living room with a knot the size of a half-dollar protruding from his forehead, their family agreed to allow us to stay with them every morning and every afternoon, Monday through Friday, plus all day in the summer.

As I reflect back to those days, I can clearly see Katie, at the age of eighteen months, walking around in Willy's cowboy boots. I can also remember walking down the gravel road to catch our local school bus and can picture the soybean fields and pastures that surrounded the Calverts' home. I can remember spending afternoons visiting with Charlotte's parents and can picture times spent at her sister's ceramic shop where I painted a mushroom canister set for Mother and a Blue Devil football player for Willy. And I also remember sharing ice-cold colas, packaged in glass bottles, with Charlotte. Since I was the oldest of all the children, Charlotte always made me feel like I was her "equal." I never remember being perceived as a child but rather as a young adult, in her eyes at least. For some odd reason, she actually trusted me to help with the "grown-up" work. She also trusted me to assist her with hanging out the clothes on the clothesline and in making lunch, which always consisted of a meal prepared Southern-style with foods like fried squash, fried okra, peas, and cornbread. Charlotte even trusted me to hold her infant child and did not overreact when I accidentally dropped Katie from my lap onto the dirt underneath the swing where I was sitting.

Looking back, I now realize how fortunate my brother and I were to have been supervised by such people of character. Unlike children who were placed in overcrowded daycare facilities, we were placed in the homes of kind people who loved us as if we were their own. For that, I will always be grateful.

Southern Colloquisms

Many of the expressions we grew up with were quite common in the rural South, while others were certainly unique. The following expressions were as common as kudzu in the rural south and were used in our households as well:

Bless your heart.

He wouldn't hit a lick at a snake.

Don't get above your raisin'.

You should've had better sense.

It's comin' up a cloud.

I reckon we'd best head out for the storm cellar.

Do you want a sup of my sweet tea?

You'd best push away from the table.

Don't act like you were raised in a barn.

Stop actin' a fool.

Hush that racket you're makin'.

Don't make me have to come in there.

Hand me that fly flap.

And then there were expressions that we associated with certain people from our hometown:

Daddy often said, "Get your education while you're young." And when we did something inappropriate, he'd respond, "You ought to be ashamed."

At Christmas, William often commented on the overly zealous neighbors and the amount of multi-colored lights they used to decorate their yards, trees, homes, and any other object they could wrap in electric lights. "That place is lit up like a beer joint," he would reply as he worried about how they managed to foot the REA power bill.

"He's got enough money to burn a wet mule," was a common phrase of William's as well as "He looks rough, like a horse that's been rode hard and put up wet."

Although William had his share of sayings, Mrs. Maggie took the cake. After her husband passed away and people tried to fix her up with another man, Mrs. Maggie replied, "Heck, I wouldn't want another husband if all his parts were made of gold, and he came equipped with his own motor."

Not only was Mrs. Maggie disinterested in dating, she also had little tolerance for people who were less than trustworthy. Therefore, when certain names of people who had seedy reputations were dropped into the conversation, she often said, "Well, he'd steal poop from a tumbleweed bug and put him on the wrong road home" and "He's not worth the bullet it would take to kill him."

And when people pressured Mrs. Maggie to retire in her seventies, she simply replied, "It's better to wear out than to rust out."

Had Mrs. Maggie lived a few more years, I believed I would have talked her in to writing this book. After all, she certainly had a way with words.

Hit a Lick at a Snake

In Detroit, Alabama, there were basically two types of people. It was a simple dichotomy. You had those that would work themselves to death and those who wouldn't hit a lick at a snake. Our parents, aunts, uncles, and grandparents would have been classified in the first category. They were all workaholics. For as long as I can remember, my parents and my friends' parents all had gardens larger than most city blocks, which they maintained with a simple garden hoe and some sweat of their brow. They also mowed their own yards with push mowers and kept the tall weeds and bushes that permeated the perimeter of the land at bay with a sling blade. They hung out clothes on the clothesline, grew most of the food their families ate, and cleaned their own houses. No family that I knew ever paid a maid to clean their house or employed a lawn service to take care of their yard. Our parents even cut down their own trees. My mother and Virginia Mae both had their own chain saws.

With the exception of mealtime, I have no memories of our parents ever sitting down. I can only picture them either working outside in the heat of the day or dead asleep at night. They were always driven to be productive with their time.

I was reminded of all of this the other day when a friend of mine mentioned that many of the sixteen-year-old boys he employs for his lawn care service just can't seem to hold out to work.

"Can't hold out to work?" I asked.

This concept was beyond my comprehension. All I could picture was my brother and Jake throwing fifty-pound hay bales onto the back of trucks for hours and pulling weeds from the soybean fields in the blistering heat of summer. And I thought about the women in our area and how they worked all day at garment factories and then came home to work in their one-acre gardens. I also thought about how these women did their own laundry, canned their own vegetables, made quilts from scraps of clothing, prepared meals for their families every night, and often stood behind a tiller to cultivate the soil in their gardens.

I can only imagine what Aunt Irene, Virginia Mae, Laura, Mrs. Maggie, and Mother would have thought about the young guys who couldn't hold out to mow yards on a riding lawn mower. Actually, I know exactly what they'd say.

"Those boys aren't fit for nothin'; they're too lazy to hit a lick at a snake."

And so, on that note, I realize I must get back to work. After all, I am my mother's daughter.

Time for Supper

According to a recent poll, approximately 25 percent of families eat together less than three times a week. This certainly wasn't the case for us. I can easily count on one hand the number of times our family went out to eat from the earliest that I can recall until the very day I went away to college. In fact, we only ate out when we were on vacation. Eating out was considered a big waste of money. According to our parents, there was "just no sense in it" since we had enough food stored away in glass Mason jars to last a lifetime.

For the most part, we ate just about any kind of vegetable imaginable, that we'd grown in our garden as well as chicken and ample helpings of bread. These were always prepared a certain way: Southern style. Okra, squash, and green tomatoes were picked fresh from the garden and were later coated in cornmeal and fried in a hot cast-iron skillet. Chicken was never broiled; it was first dipped in buttermilk, then coated in flour, and then fried. Peas, corn, and green beans were well-cooked, not steamed, and were coated with plenty of Crisco and salt for taste. Fried apples pies and blackberry cobblers were baked using plenty of sugar with fruits we'd grown and picked ourselves. Sweet potatoes were baked in a cast-iron skillet for over an hour and were later coated in butter. And you could always count on the fact that an iron skillet of cornbread and a pan of biscuits would be served at both dinner and supper. Like other rural areas in the South, low-fat meals were basically unheard of around our house.

Breakfast was no exception. Most mornings we'd awaken to the smell of bacon and sausage frying in an iron skillet, country-fried ham, scrambled eggs, grits, and Mother's own homemade drop biscuits. At the table, we'd smother our biscuits with homemade blackberry preserves and spoonfuls of real butter so that the mixture oozed out all sides. With the exception of cereal on a few occasions, breakfast rarely came out of a box.

Although we ate meat for breakfast, steaks were somewhat of a rarity around our house. In fact, the only steaks we had were hamburger steaks fried in a cast-iron skillet, coated in salt. But things were quite different around the Cash household. Since the Cash family owned cattle, their freezers were usually packed to the brim with beef from the local meat processing plant referred to as the Sulligent Quick Freeze. I still remember looking into their freezer and noticing the various cuts of beef individually wrapped in butcher paper, stamped with purple ink. You could always count on getting a succulent steak when you had supper with the Cash family.

And, if you had dinner over at Mrs. Maggie's, you were in for a special treat. Each Sunday, following our morning worship service at Detroit First Baptist, Mrs. Maggie and Laura prepared what we always referred to as a spread. Everything on the dinner table was homemade. Nothing came out of a cardboard box or a store-bought can for that matter. On most Sundays, we'd have a smorgasbord of fried chicken, turkey and dressing, mashed potatoes and gravy, baked ham, turnip greens, baked beans, fried squash, macaroni and cheese, green beans, black-eyed peas, fried okra, strawberry cake, banana pudding, sweet-potato pie, and the best melt-in-your-mouth rolls made in the South.

As I write this, I find myself wishing the next time I'm at a fast food restaurant, the #2 combo would be some of Mrs. Maggie's fried chicken, mashed potatoes, fried okra, rolls, and a some sweet tea. Now *that* would be worth supersizing.

The Phoenix

Here in Athens, Alabama, the average one-acre lot costs about fifty thousand. Some lots in the one-acre range cost as much as one hundred thousand, while others are considerably less. In some parts of the country, this would be considered a real bargain, a steal so to speak. That would not be the case in Detroit, Alabama.

In Detroit, people pay more for a freezer than they do for an acre of land. For five hundred dollars, one can easily obtain an acre of land, if you can find anyone willing to part with it.

Although the cost of living is affordable, the tragic thing is that most of the industries have packed their bags and moved away. Many of the townspeople, in need of work, have had no choice but to do the same. There is little left here to do other than farm or teach. And you only need so many teachers, when the population is dwindling away.

Oddly enough, a part of me likes the fact that my hometown is still quiet, untouched by the franchises that permeate so many areas, yet another part of me is saddened that this area's population has actually decreased in recent years. And deep down, I know that unless something drastic happens the trend will continue.

I can only hope that industries will somehow return, so that the town can be renewed once again, just like the phoenix that burned itself to death and later rose up out of the ashes and found itself regenerated, whole again.

PART III
Interwoven Threads

Women in our area made quilts from scraps of material that once served as items of clothing or once hung in the windows. Actually, that's what made them special. When you'd look at a quilt made by one of our mothers or grandmothers, you'd often find pieces of the past. What was once a shirt later served as an integral part of the patch-work quilt. And, on many occasions, not only would you notice scraps from your own household, but you'd find scraps from other households as well. This sharing of fabric scraps was as common as the sharing of items grown in the garden. The result was a quilt that was woven together to reflect the lives of many people. Some fabrics were reminders of happy times; others were reminders of hard times. Nonetheless, all the elements came together to form a beautiful unique piece of art.

A Call to Worship

Let your light shine before men in such a way that they may see your good works, and glorify your Father who is in heaven. Matthew 5:16, New American Standard

Detroit First Baptist Church, with its red brick walls and tall white steeple, is nestled along Highway 17, in the heart of Detroit, Alabama, directly between the First National Bank and the Detroit Grocery. Like other churches in our area, within its walls are solid salt-of-the-earth people who will tell you their opinion in a heartbeat and live each day exactly as they preach. Most of its fifty or so members are there each Sunday morning, Sunday evening, and believe it or not, even on Wednesday nights.

It is somewhat fitting that Detroit First Baptist would be located in the center of our small town, since its effects radiated out into the community and into our lives, like spokes attached to the hub of a wheel. And like spokes that share the same wheel, the members here share in the many facets of life. When children are born, the women of the church are there to host baby showers and to marvel at the joy of a new arrival. When mothers are sick, they will step in and bring pans full of homemade turkey and dressing, mashed potatoes, baked beans, and batches of banana pudding packed in some airtight Tupperware. And when death takes a loved one, the members here not only attend the funeral and assist the grieving family with their everyday needs like cleaning and cooking, but they take the time to visit, to listen, and to offer words of sympathy. The members here have perfected the art of demonstrating unconditional love for their fellow man.

The members of Detroit First Baptist, like others in our community, are godly members who know their Bible, both inside and out, and more importantly, live by its principles each day. They are people you can trust, whose handshake and word mean as much as a written contract. They are steadfast and compassionate and are willing to take on leadership roles in the church and in their community. They are sacrificial people who would gladly lend a helping hand to anyone in need.

I know this because I grew up here. In a fifty or so member church, you know people, well. I remember distinct characteristics about each person and can still picture where each member sat. Along the middle aisle on the very front pew, you'd find Mr. Roy, Ken's father, who at the age of 96 still managed to attend church every time the door was open. I can still picture Mr. Roy's smile and can still feel his handshake with his callused hands, formed by years of hard labor on the farm. And I well remember how, each Sunday, Mr. Roy would ask about my family's well-being. Mr. Roy was a saint.

On the far right of the same pew where Mr. Roy sat was Mr. Leon, our former Sunday school teacher. Mr. Leon always sat near the edge so he could prop up his elbow on the arm of the pew and would occasionally nod at the preacher and yell out a good "Amen!" every now and then. Mr. Leon, bless his heart, was also famous for his marathon benediction prayers. Whenever the preacher called on Mr. Leon to pray, we young folks would glance at each other and exchange tired looks. Then we'd close our eyes and shift our weight from one leg to the other while Mr. Leon led us in a word of prayer for what seemed like an eternity.

A row or so back from Mr. Leon sat Laura and Ken, who were positioned in the center of the middle aisle and were among only a handful of couples that actually sat next to each other. I can still hear Ken's benediction prayers and can remember how he served as a deacon at Detroit First Baptist for over four decades. I always admired Ken for practicing what he believed and for possessing such wisdom in rearing his children, in dealing with financial matters, in managing his farm, and in taking care of his parents and his wife. And when I think of Ken, I'm always reminded that he was not only intelligent, but more importantly, he was wise. I can still hear Ken's wife, Laura, as she stood and sang the classic hymns, all by heart, during each service. Laura has been a member of the choir and has taught Sunday school for as long as I can remember. And I'd put her knowledge of the Bible up against any seminary graduate, any day of the week.

Near Laura and Ken sat Daddy. He sat near the edge of one of the middle pews. I can still picture Daddy, all dressed up in his Sunday best, holding a hymnal and smiling as he sang each word. Although Daddy loved music, he was always too shy to sing as a member of the choir but went to choir practice nonetheless and sang along with them from his place on the wooden pew. And whenever he got a chance, he'd attend one of those all-day singing events where they would sing for hours on Sunday afternoons out of thin paperback hymnals filled with music written in shape notes. On Sunday mornings, you could always count on the fact that Daddy's shirts would be starched stiff as a board, his pants would be perfectly creased, and his shoes would be shined to high gloss, like mirrors. And most importantly, you could count on the fact that he'd be there, in his spot on one of the middle pews.

Over on the right side of the church sat Mother, along with Mrs. Belle and Mrs. Evelyn. Behind these ladies sat Clint, who at 6'6" was simply a teddy bear with a big heart, all wrapped up in a gladiator's body. Beside Clint sat his wife Katie, who received more than her share of talents. Katie could play the piano, teach Sunday school and WMU, and direct the Christmas plays all simultaneously, like a master conductor directing a symphony orchestra. And one row behind Clint and Katie sat most of the young folks my age including Jessica and her brother Jake, Lori, Greg, my brother Willy and me, and the Mitchell brothers.

And when I picture the young people I grew up with, I often think back to our annual Christmas play where I, for some odd reason, usually ended up playing the role of Mary and Greg took on the role of Joseph. Looking back, I think this was because Jessica was the only one from our group who could play the piano. And so, she sat on the piano bench and tickled the ivories while we stood on stage and tried our best to make our parents proud. Willy, Jake, and Phillip, bless their hearts, always ended up as shepherds. Their costumes were consistently the same each year. I can still picture them walking down the church's aisle wearing their bathrobes with fluffy bath towels tightly wound around their foreheads.

As I think back to this time, I can also picture the time the deacons of the church entrusted Willy and Jake to pick out a Christmas tree for our church's sanctuary. I can still visualize the look on Mr. Roy's face when the guys drove up with an evergreen that was at least thirty feet tall. "Good night alive boys! Can't you measure no better than that?" he exclaimed.

I can still see the two of them sawing away at the tree's base, time and time again, until they finally ended up bringing in the top nine feet or so of the tree into the front doors of the church. To my knowledge, that's the last time those two jokers were asked to be in charge of the Christmas tree.

I also remember singing in the church's choir under the direction of our Minister of Music, Randy Mitchell. Since our church was small, we didn't have to exactly audition for the choir. Any willing, able-bodied person was permitted to stand up at the front of the church and make a joyful noise. This was, at least, what I did. I couldn't sing worth a lick. But Randy encouraged me and the other choir members to sing out, in spite of our talent, or the lack thereof. I can still hear Willy, Jake, Phillip, and Greg as they sang various Southern gospel songs. Although they didn't exactly sing bass, like the songs intended, it never seemed to matter. Our parents and the rest of the congregation would just smile and occasionally nod in rhythm, like they were listening to the Florida Boys quartet.

I remember how summers were spent at the softball fields, watching our team compete in the church softball leagues. The Goodwin family and a lady named Minnie made sure that we were taken to all the games and were entertained along the way. And I remember how they would make us laugh and would let us listen to the latest top 40 hits on the way to and from the games.

I also remember Vacation Bible School. Held in summer, this was an annual event, which drew in children from all over Detroit. The format was usually pretty consistent from year to year. We'd start off with a general assembly in our sanctuary where we would recite the pledge to the American flag, to the Christian flag, and to the Bible. Next, we were dismissed to our classrooms where we learned about famous Biblical characters like Moses, Isaac, Joseph, David, Daniel, Ruth, and Esther, just to name a few.

After our lesson, we'd have refreshments outside on the cement tables covered with a myriad of tablecloths. Along the cement tables were cookies, some of which were homemade by Mrs. Belle and Mrs. Evelyn. There also were gobs of thin petal-shaped shortbread cookies, purchased in bulk, to feed the hungry masses. And, of course, there were gallons of lemonade, enough to quench the thirst of about sixty or so children.

Following our refreshment break, we'd go back to our rooms for craft time. We'd design objects out of paper bags, paint ceramic crosses, glue and paint macaroni to tissue boxes, and tap into our creative side. Vacation Bible School would culminate on Friday night with a special program where each class would perform and share something they'd learned that week. Here, in front of our parents and the rest of the congregation, we tried to recite the verses we'd committed to memory as well as some new information we'd learned during that special week of Vacation Bible School.

I also remember other annual events like Old Fashion Sunday. This event was held once a year, in early October. On this day, men wore overalls, women wore long cotton dresses and bonnets, and we always had dinner on the grounds.

Dinner on the grounds was held directly following our morning church services. Dinner, like most areas in the South, was at noon; supper was what we ate at night. Whenever this event rolled around, the ladies from our church would first cover the cement tables, which rested underneath massive oak trees, with linens and would arrange these tablecloths like a row of pretty cotton dresses. Once the tablecloths were in place, the ladies of the church brought out platters of their favorite homemade entrees. These homemade goods included mouthwatering foods such as turkey and dressing, fried chicken, green beans, fried okra, cream corn, fried squash, turnip greens, black-eyed peas, pound cake, banana pudding, apple pie, coconut cake, and gallons of sweet tea.

Once the entrees were perfectly arranged on the tables, with the desserts in one area and vegetables in another, the congregation formed a line and filled their paper plates until they overflowed with a myriad of delicious home-baked goods. Usually, the men ended up going through the food line first. Then the children were next in line with their mothers walking right beside them, spooning out small servings onto their paper plates. After filling up their paper plates with a hearty sampling of the homemade foods, the men would all congregate together in one spot with the women standing in another, usually under the shade of one of the oak trees, laughing and sharing stories. While their parents and grandparents enjoyed some moments of fellowship, the boys from our church usually took this opportunity to play in the drainage ditch that was nestled alongside the church's property. Understandably, our mothers despised this ditch. This made it all the more appealing to my brother and the other boys in our congregation, who always seemed to emerge from the ditch with their dirt-clod battle wounds invariably spread across their Sunday shirts.

Around two o'clock or so in the afternoon, once everyone had finally had enough to eat, the ladies gave away their leftovers to each other, ensuring that each family left with an adequate sampling of food from the day's event. Once the tablecloths were folded and placed in the trunks of each car, we returned home for a few hours and then returned promptly to Detroit First Baptist at five-thirty for our Sunday night service, still full from our earlier feast.

The memories I have of Detroit First Baptist are dear ones. Here, I witnessed firsthand the spirit of true compassion, dedication, and integrity. I hope in being so close to these elements that somehow these qualities rubbed off on me, even if just a little bit. After all, that's what church is all about.

Teachers

A teacher affects eternity; he can never tell
where his influence stops.
~ Henry Brooks Adams

Recently, I heard verses from the song *Amazing Grace* during our morning worship service. For a moment my mind flashed back to my childhood, and a knot began to form in my throat as I thought back to a time at Detroit First Baptist, when Mr. Leon was still living. I remember how much he loved that particular song. I can still hear the enthusiasm in the tone of his voice, as he would exclaim, "Let's sing every stanza!" On most occasions, we sang only the first, second, and last stanzas, so this request was out of the ordinary and thus a special one. In my mind, I can still hear him singing that infamous song from our hymnal, just like it all sounded decades ago. From the tone in his voice, it was obvious that the words touched his heart. If the hymns we grew up with are sung in heaven, I'm certain Mr. Leon's making that request at this very moment.

I can still picture Mr. Leon. His hair was the color of new fallen snow and his tanned face revealed that he had worked outside for most of his life by the sweat of his brow. Mr. Leon was our Sunday school teacher during our formative years as we tried to make sense of what being a Christian was all about. As I recall, we asked him to explain the plan of salvation. We'd heard about this concept at home and from the pulpit, but we still needed some clarification. The exact words are no longer retrievable, but I do remember he explained things in a way that a young person could readily understand. He was instrumental in helping my friends and me come to a personal decision about our faith. For that, I will always be grateful.

I have vivid memories of other Sunday school teachers as well. They, too, molded us into the individuals we are today. During our final years of high school, Laura served as our Sunday school teacher. She was and still is a true Bible scholar. I have always been in awe of her knowledge and understanding of both the Old and New Testaments. I often tell her that she's forgotten more than I will ever know. Her husband, Ken, whose discernment of the Bible is also remarkable, served as our teacher during my college years. I remember many of the lessons Ken taught and also remember that he not only possessed knowledge, but he clearly had something even more valuable…his wisdom.

Randy was the brave one who agreed to serve as our Sunday school teacher during our hormonal teenage years. Randy somehow managed to deal with our group on a weekly basis, without losing his sanity. It was always obvious that he took enormous pride in preparing a host of questions that forced us to think critically and analyze various aspects of the Bible.

Randy's wife, Emily, taught our class when we were around the age of eleven. Emily was a kind soft-spoken woman who always had a smile on her face. She had a gentle demeanor and somehow dealt with us without ever raising her voice. I'll never forget some of the Biblical stories that Emily shared with us and how she would blush, on occasion, when we'd ask certain questions. I remember how she would occasionally reply, "Well, you might want to ask your parents to explain that to you," when we'd ask about certain terminology sometimes used in telling the story of David and Bathsheba. Emily was a saint.

Anne, bless her heart, was also a saint and taught our class during the elementary school years. She always accepted us as rambunctious children and somehow managed to just smile at us in spite of our inattentiveness at times. I remember how she would gear a lesson to our short attention spans and then allow time for us to play a few board games. Anne, of course, was one of our favorite teachers.

After having served as a teacher in the public schools for over a decade, I now hold a special place in my heart for teachers, especially those who choose to work with young people. And I have a true appreciation for the sacrifices my Sunday school teachers made. I know it wasn't easy planning lessons and studying the scriptures each and every week, especially for a group of youngsters like ourselves, but I am grateful that they agreed to accept this role, mainly because teachers do more than affect the here and now.

I'm certainly looking forward to seeing my former teachers again. And I want to be sure and thank Mr. Leon for his influence as a teacher, for how he affected eternity. Most of all, I'm looking forward to hearing him exclaim, "Let's sing *Amazing Grace*…every stanza."

Driving Mrs. Maggie

I am quite certain Mrs. Maggie could drive. I remember seeing a car parked in her garage for as long as I can remember. It's just that whenever Mrs. Maggie went with us on a shopping trip, her daughter Laura always did the driving. As a young teenager, I had the privilege of going on several of these shopping trips with Jessica, Laura, and Mrs. Maggie. Even though almost three decades have passed since that time, I remember many of the trips as though it all happened yesterday.

The nearest shopping mall was about fifty miles from our hometown of Detroit, Alabama. So "going to town" was an all day event. On days that we ventured off to Columbus, Mississippi, Mrs. Maggie would insist that we leave by nine o'clock at the very latest, so we'd be sure and be among the first customers to enter the doors of the shopping mall, which opened promptly at ten on Saturday mornings.

Mrs. Maggie always made the one-hour journey an entertaining one. Much to Laura's dismay, Mrs. Maggie's colorful language and original phrases were a hoot and were quite educational to us as teenagers.

Some of her famous sayings about people who would not accept responsibility would include: "They're scum. Just pure scum" and "He's so crooked they'll have to just screw that ole joker into the ground."

When she would occasionally get upset with her husband Wesley, she'd shake her head and say, "Wes can't do anything. He can't even pour water out of a boot."

Laura would invariably glance over to Mrs. Maggie and yell, "Mother!"

And whenever Laura would get in a tizzy about Jessica's dating, Mrs. Maggie would calmly reply, "Laura, the president already has a wife." Mrs. Maggie would then glance at us in the backseat with a mischievous grin, like a cat that had just been naughty and swallowed a canary.

Mrs. Maggie also took along a stockpile of snacks for our journey, like we were going on some sort of an extended vacation. We'd have sausage and made-from-scratch biscuits as well as metal tins filled with peanut brittle, fried apple pies, and tea cakes placed between sheets of wax paper, just to name a few. And there were no limits. We could eat as much of these delicious home-baked goods our stomachs could hold as we made our journey over to Columbus.

Once we arrived, we'd usually head over to the women's department in McRae's, or on a few occasions over to Ruth's department store located in downtown Columbus. Mrs. Maggie was especially fond of beautiful clothes and often said, "If I can't be skinny, I'll just decorate myself." So she'd spend the day meticulously perusing the clothing racks in search of the perfect additions to her wardrobe. Mrs. Maggie was always in tune with the latest fashions and also had an eye for just the right accessories.

A couple of hours later we'd make our way over to Morrison's restaurant for lunch. Here, we would make our selections from the smorgasbord of foods, with Jessica predictably choosing their macaroni and cheese. Once we'd finished with lunch, we would head out again, like hunters pursuing game during the last week of hunting season.

Mrs. Maggie had as much stamina as Jessica. If it had been left up to Mrs. Maggie, we would have stayed at the mall until the last shop closed. Not Laura. Around six o'clock, Laura would have finally had enough and would literally drag Mrs. Maggie, out of the mall, like a child from a toy store.

On the way home, Mrs. Maggie would insist that we stop for a snack. We never had to worry when Mrs. Maggie was around. She always made sure we didn't go hungry, not even for a moment. We'd stop and order milkshakes so thick we'd have to scoop out the contents with a spoon. Not only did we have milkshakes, but Mrs. Maggie would also pass around bags of candy and potato chips that she'd purchased that day along the aisles of Wal-Mart. As we made the one-hour journey back to Detroit, we could count on Mrs. Maggie to not only provide us with food but to entertain us all the way home. I'll never forget how she'd make us laugh until our sides ached as we listened to her original phrases, like we were sitting through some sort of stand-up comedy act.

Mrs. Maggie passed away on Valentine's Day at the age of 82. She was like a grandmother to me. I miss her voice and her distinctive laughter. I miss her comical sayings. I miss how she loved life. I'm sure that at this moment she's entertaining people in heaven, and if she's allowed to do some cooking up there, she's serving up quite a feast.

Family Traditions

Southerners love traditions. My family was no exception...

Each year, the third Sunday in September, my father's side of the family gathered together for a reunion. When I was a child, this reunion was always held at the Sulligent Lake in Lamar County. As I understand it, this location was chosen primarily because the area was equipped with a pavilion near the water, which offered some shelter from the oppressive heat and humidity.

Underneath the pavilion were some sturdy tables, made from cement. Once my aunts arrived, these particular tables were quickly covered with cotton tablecloths and were filled with delicious desserts, garden-grown vegetables, homemade breads, and fried chicken.

I can still picture each table. One table was designated solely for desserts. Like most celebrations in the South, this table was lined with fresh coconut cakes, banana pudding, blackberry cobblers, sweet potato pies, tea cakes, and fried apple pies, all made from scratch. Fried chicken and baked ham were placed at the end of another table, next to the plastic plates, cups, forks, and knives. Along the middle table you'd find fried okra, fried squash, black-eyed peas, green beans, turnip greens, deviled eggs, and a bowl of homegrown tomatoes.

My aunts, like most Southern women raised during the Depression Era, could cook. There was no chance you'd find fast food or store-bought items along these tables. Everything was either made from scratch or was grown in one of their many gardens.

Once these home-cooked foods were organized and meticulously sorted by type, family members were beckoned to gather together for a word of prayer. After the prayer, we were allowed to make our way down the sides of each table and place samples of each item on our plastic plates, lest we would offend one of our aunts.

After our plates were overflowing with food, members of the family would then gather together to eat. Men sat together under one of the oak trees, women gathered together underneath the pavilion, and those of us who were old enough to eat by ourselves gathered together over by the lake.

Once we'd eaten as much as our stomachs could hold, we would play chase by the banks of the lake. In doing so, we had to promise to be careful. Most of all, we had to vow that we would not push any of our cousins into the lake's waters. Although I've forgotten many things about our family reunions, I especially remember talking with Grandfather Rye and being mesmerized by the gold pocket watch that he always had with him. This particular watch was somewhat larger than a fifty-cent piece and was attached to his Sunday overalls on a long gold chain. I can still picture him opening up the watch like a locket, allowing me to run my fingers over the glass dial and later closing the gold case with my fingers.

I can also picture Aunt Jo, Uncle Cecil, and Aunt Louise with their outgoing personalities, hugging everyone and talking up a storm. I can picture Aunt Nellie, the epitome of a Southern Belle, with her sweet demeanor and soft laughter. I can picture Daddy talking with his brother Cletis, whose calm, easy-going personality was much like my father's. I can picture Uncle Lowell smoking a pipe while he talked with Uncle Russell. And I can picture my Aunt Maxine and Aunt Ruby arranging all of the foods in a meticulous manner, making sure everything was perfect.

I have similar snapshots in my mind of family reunions with my mother's relatives. These were held on a regular basis out at Aunt Irene's. I can still picture all six of Mother's sisters (Louise, Geraldine, Edilene, Lorene, Bertie Mae, and Lillie Rea) and my Uncle Lester as well as several first and second cousins all gathered around tables filled with a plethora of home-cooked foods. And I can still taste the freshly-squeezed lemonade and coconut cakes made by Aunt Irene and the lemon icebox pie made by Aunt Bert. Most of all, I can still hear the sound of their laughter as they retold stories of their youth.

I hope these snapshots and sounds remain with me for years to come and that this written account will also help others to recall their own memories of family traditions.

More than Enough

Money wasn't exactly abundant around our household. Since both of my parents were born to sharecroppers during the Great Depression and never had the financial means to pursue their education, they had few choices when it came to supporting their families. They choose to work at a local pants factory known as Detroit Slacks. Here, they earned only minimum wage. That only goes so far, even with the best money management skills. To make ends meet, we ate primarily from the garden, took very few family vacations, and learned to make do with just the basic necessities. We even did most of our Christmas shopping at the *S & H Green Stamps* store, paying for our gifts with small paper booklets we'd filled with adhesive stamps.

Since our family's average yearly income was less than fifteen thousand, we qualified for the Free Lunch program at our school. But my daddy would have nothing of the sort. Whenever we brought home the forms to see if we qualified, he'd toss these papers into the garbage and say, "We will pay for your lunch. We'll just cut corners somewhere else." And so, we lived rather simply, but took pride in the few material things we possessed.

Books and magazines were few and far between, almost nonexistent. All I can remember in our house was a huge family version of the *Holy Bible* that sat on an end table and housed bills and just about any other piece of scrap paper that Mother chose to press between its pages. And we each had our own personal Bible we carried to church each Sunday and Wednesday night. We also had monthly issues of *Progressive Farmer,* and copies of the local weekly newspapers: *The Lamar Democrat* and the *Lamar Leader.* Although we didn't have any children's literature, we did have a set of *World Book Encyclopedias*, published in 1970, which I've never been able to part with, even to this day. At the time, we were keenly aware of the fact that Mother and Daddy had made a huge sacrifice to purchase these for us. And so, my brother and I spent hours carefully perusing the glossy pages of each encyclopedia as we read everything from facts about an abacus to the topic of zoology.

In addition to the lack of print in our home, Mother and Daddy rarely bought themselves anything new. Mother's closet, unlike most ladies, consisted of only a few items, most of which had been purchased at discount stores. Daddy's closet was much the same. I'll never forget how at Christmas he would say, "Please don't buy me anything. Just save your money. I have more than enough." Mother and Daddy were masters at pretending like they didn't need or want material things, although I'm sure they did this to protect our feelings and to use what money they had to provide for our needs, the best way they knew how.

My parents cut costs in other ways. The house was cooled (I use that term loosely) with portable fans, and we dried our clothes on the clothesline. Daddy even opted not to have a telephone, so we could pocket that money as well. And I can still picture Mother reusing aluminum foil and peanut butter jars and saving scraps of cloth to use for future quilts.

Although children were often ridiculed for not having certain material possessions, my experience was quite different. My friends, who clearly possessed much more than my family, accepted me as well as my family with open arms. Somehow it really didn't matter to them that our home had less than nine hundred square feet or that our clothes didn't always match. I never remember them saying anything about the fact that we had to hang our clothes on the clothesline since we didn't own a dryer, and I never remember them commenting on the fact that our one television set was tiny and only projected in black and white. And they never complained about the stifling air that we circulated around the house with fans, since we couldn't afford an air conditioner. In fact, I can't recall a time that they ever made a condescending remark.

Even though my friends never said anything, I was always embarrassed that my family didn't have certain material things. I remember staring in awe at the neatly stacked clothes in Jessica's closet, filled with matching sets of shirts and shorts and gazing in wonder at the chandelier that hung over her four-poster bed. I can still picture their living room with its upholstered French Provincial furniture, elaborate window treatments, and piano. At my home, there were no custom window treatments (just simple valances purchased from discount stores), no French Provincial (just a sofa and chairs covered with imitation leather called Naugahyde), few matching sets of clothing, and certainly no chandeliers.

As a child, I always found myself comparing what my family owned with others. Looking back, I can remember little things like envying Jessica's dollhouse, the one with the three stories and an elevator. At my house, I did well to own a couple of Barbie dolls, so we just had to improvise and pretend that my bookshelf was a Manhattan apartment for Barbie and Ken. I was always embarrassed that at Jessica's we were able to play in a real playhouse, while at my house we had to play in a playhouse crafted from scrap tin and discarded curtains. Jessica never complained. She just went along with my make-do toys. Even though I was well aware of where my family stood in the class-system hierarchy, Jessica, Clint, Jake, Grace, Kathryn, and their families accepted us wholeheartedly and pretended not to notice.

Although my friends and their families accepted us for who we were and not for what we had, poverty still had an adverse effect on me. As I thought about what my family had from a material standpoint, I often felt like I was less of a person. This was a feeling I imposed on myself. I can't blame anyone else for this. This feeling is a difficult one to overcome, even as an adult.

I guess that's because poverty is like a deep puncture wound. Although the wound may heal, the scar is permanent and serves as a constant reminder of the pain. The only difference is that the scars created by poverty aren't always visible; these scars reside deep inside the person and take even longer to heal. But I suppose we can learn something from our scars, if we choose to do so. Sometimes in remembering the pain, we will vow to do anything to avoid facing it again. And sometimes these vows cause us to be more productive, more compassionate, and more determined.

In spite of this, I often wonder why God allows people to be born in impoverished situations. From my perspective, it really doesn't seem quite fair, but I suppose God can see the whole picture, and I cannot. Ultimately, though, I'm thankful he allowed me to be born into a home and into an area where people accepted me unconditionally and made me feel loved. I now realize…I had more than enough.

The Homeplace

Where we love is home. Home that our feet may leave,
but not our hearts.
~ Oliver Wendell Holmes

A few years back, my brother and I sold our childhood home along with an acre of land. No one prepared me for how difficult that decision would be. I had no idea that I'd grieve, like I'd lost a member of my immediate family. I suppose it's because throughout my childhood our family never moved, not even once. And although our house was small and was located on a remote gravel road, it was our home…the only home we'd ever known.

I dream about our childhood house every now and then. Well, to be honest, I dream about it at least once a month. Guess that's just my way of dealing with this loss. Right after we sold the house, the dreams were pretty much the same. I'd dream that Willy and I would spend the night over at Mother's and then wake up and realize it wasn't our home any more. In these dreams, we'd wake up the next morning and scurry about, cleaning up the house and making the beds so the new owners wouldn't realize we'd trespassed. Lately, my dreams have changed. I now dream we all spend the night over at the homeplace by making reservations with the new owners, like it's some sort of vacation retreat. I suppose this shift in the dream world means that I'm making some progress.

It's just difficult to give up the one place that holds so many memories. And I'm finding that at my age, I miss it more than ever. I'm finding that I now miss simple things that I honestly took for granted as a child. I miss the serenity, the peace and quiet of the country. I miss being lulled to sleep by the sounds of crickets and katydids and the bubbling sound of the creek. I miss the pitch-black night where stars shine clearly like silver sequins pressed against black fabric. I miss the sweet gum and oak trees that Willy and I climbed as children. I miss being able to walk out around in the backyard and pick fresh strawberries, luscious red tomatoes, and grapes right off the vine and to eat them all, there on the spot. I miss being able to feast on bushels of blackberries alongside our gravel road. I miss the tart taste of the huckleberries that grew on bushes, the taste of sweet muscadines that grew on twisted vines deep in our woods, and the taste of water drawn from our well. I miss the sight of apple slices drying in the sun on top of newspapers and the taste of these slices once they're baked in some of mom's fried apple pies. And I miss the smell of honeysuckles.

I can still visualize the view perfectly. I can still picture our small home nestled in the heart of forty acres, safely enveloped by a myriad of trees. I can still picture the grapevine that Daddy planted over near the well, the shallow creek that once carried away some of our belongings, the garden filled with tall stalks of corn and rows of beans and patches of strawberries and watermelons, and our small orchard of June apples. I can still picture the massive oak tree over near the mailbox, the hill behind the house that we slid down in metal tubs whenever our land was dusted with winter snow, and the storm cellar where Mother often sent me during tornado season in the middle of the night. I can still picture Willy riding his purple and white bicycle across the front yard, Mother hanging out clothes on the clothesline, and Daddy breaking up the garden with the tiller. And I can still picture our family walking around our forty acres in search of the perfect evergreen to bring home and decorate with cheap silver garland and colored lights. I hope I'll always be able to visualize these snapshots in my mind.

I do worry that one of these days I'll forget. My grandfather, John Daniel Rye, passed away at the age of 98, after suffering with Alzheimer's disease for over a decade. I often wonder if by some twist of fate I've inherited this debilitating gene. I wonder what it must feel like to have your memories disappear, like erasing a chalkboard filled with information. Perhaps writing these childhood memories will help me to remember what the homeplace was like, especially when I'm older and the inevitable eraser begins to wipe these memories away.

Epilogue

I suppose most towns resemble a tapestry in that each is made up of individual parts or threads that are interwoven, forming its unique character. The tapestry of Detroit was certainly similar to the tapestries of other towns in that it was a typical town made up of families, a few businesses, churches, and a post office, elements that all affect each other one way or another. But the tapestry of Detroit was also quite different. Here, we never had to worry with traffic, with next door neighbors, with waiting in lines, with missing an exit, with road rage, or with crowded malls. Life in rural Alabama was rather calm. The pace was slow and the people were friendly.

I'm sure that today when people drive through my hometown they perceive it differently than I do. They probably see the underside of the tapestry, the side with knots and threads connecting in a chaotic fashion, the side that no one wants to display. But when I go home to visit, I suppose I look beyond the closed businesses and dilapidated buildings. I project an image onto an imaginary screen that's been stored in my long-term memory. I see the front of the tapestry. The picture I see in my mind is how things were thirty or so odd years ago.

As I reflect on my childhood, I now realize that I was actually fortunate to have been one of the threads in this particular town's tapestry. But, to be completely honest, I haven't always felt that way. As a young person growing up in rural Alabama, I didn't appreciate the gardens that spanned acres, the massive farms, and the remoteness of it all. I felt like a square peg in a round hole. I wanted more. I wanted to attend Broadway shows, to listen to symphony orchestras, and to shop in the finest stores.

Today, since I now live near Huntsville, I have these opportunities, yet I now find myself reflecting on my childhood and appreciating the uniqueness of my hometown. I suppose, in some ways, I'm a bit homesick. In fact, there are days when I wish I could simply do as Dorothy and click my ruby slippers together and become magically transported back home. But deep down, I know that even if I did go back, home would not be the same.

Even in Lamar County, things change. Many of the adults that were so instrumental in my life are now deceased. Therefore, when I visit my hometown, I no longer have the ability to drop by and visit with Mr. Leon, Mrs. Evelyn, Mr. Wes, Mrs. Maggie, Mrs. Belle, Mr. Roy, or with my own parents, for that matter.

This reality has never quite seemed real to me. It just doesn't seem possible that people who were such an integral part of my life are now gone. I suppose it's just one of those things I really can't wrap my mind around.

One thing I do think about is how fortunate I am in the sense that my childhood friends and I still keep in touch on a regular basis. It's amazing, actually. Somehow we've managed to maintain our close friendships for over three decades. It's as though our lives became intertwined early on and have continued to grow together, much like braided twigs that have woven together to form an inseparable vine.

And so, we make it a point to get together on a regular basis. Whenever we do, we inevitably reflect back on our favorite childhood memories and are awestruck that a town, with a population of less than three hundred, could hold so many memories. So now, as an adult, I realize that Dorothy, in *The Wizard of Oz*, was right when she said, "There's no place like home." Detroit, Alabama is indeed a special place. And I am proud to call it my hometown.

978-0-595-41080-4
0-595-41080-4